Guide to

Managerial Communication

Effective Business Writing and Speaking

Fifth Edition

by Mary Munter
Amos Tuck School of Business
Dartmouth College

PRENTICE HALL
Upper Saddle River, New Jersey 07458

For Julet, Laurlet, and Paolucci

Editor-in-Chief: Natalie Anderson
VP/Editorial Director: James Boyd
Assistant Editor: Kristen Imperatore
Editorial Assistant: Sue Galle
Director of Development: Steve Deitmer
Marketing Manager: Debbie Clare
Production Editor: Lynda P. Hansler
Associate Managing Editor: Judy Leale
Manufacturing Buyer: Diane Peirano
Manufacturing Supervisor: Arnold Vila
Manufacturing Manager: Vincent Scelta
Design Director: Patricia Smythe
Interior Design: Ann France
Art Director: Jayne Conte
Cover Design: Joe Sengotta
Composition: Preparé / Emilcomp

Library of Congress Cataloging–in–Publication Data
Munter, Mary.
Guide to managerial communication: effective business writing and speaking / by Mary Munter. — 5th ed.
p. cm.
Includes bibliographical references and index.
ISBN 0-13-013381-7
1. Business communication. 2. Communication in management.
I. Title. II. Title: Managerial communication.
HF5718.M86 1999 99-23920
658.4'5—dc21 CIP

Prentice-Hall International (UK) Limited, *London*
Prentice-Hall of Australia Pty. Limited, *Sydney*
Prentice-Hall Canada, Inc., *Toronto*
Prentice-Hall Hispanoamericana, S.A., *Mexico*
Prentice-Hall of India Private Limited, *New Delhi*
Prentice-Hall of Japan, Inc., *Tokyo*
Prentice-Hall Pte. Ltd., *Singapore*
Editora Prentice-Hall do Brasil, Ltda., *Rio de Janeiro*

Printed in the United States of America

10 9 8 7 6 5 4 3 2 1

Contents

Introduction

HOW THIS BOOK CAN HELP YOU

If you are facing a specific managerial communication problem, turn to the relevant part of this book for guidance. For example:

- You're speaking or writing to a new group of people. How can you enhance your credibility? How can you appeal to them?
- You can't get started on a writing project. How can you overcome writer's block?
- The thought of giving that presentation next week is making you nervous. What can you do to relax?
- In making your case, you don't know whether to start with your recommendation or to build up to it. Which is more persuasive?
- Your new computer programs can create terrific visual aids and writing formats. How can you get the most out of them?
- Your boss is returning your memos and reports to you to rewrite. How can you organize your ideas? How can you express yourself more succinctly?
- You're wasting time at meetings. How can you get more accomplished?

If you don't have a specific question, but need general guidelines, procedures, and techniques, read through this entire book. For example:

- You would like a framework for thinking strategically about all managerial communication.
- You would like to know more about the process of writing and editing more efficiently.

- You would like a step-by-step procedure for preparing an oral presentation.

If you are taking a professional training course, a college course, a workshop, or a seminar, use this book as a reference.

- You may very well be a good communicator already. You would like, however, to polish and refine your managerial writing and speaking skills by taking a course or seminar.

WHO CAN USE THIS BOOK

This book is written for you if you need to speak or write in a managerial, business, government, or professional context—that is, if you need to achieve results with and through other people. You probably already know these facts:

- *You spend most of your time at work communicating.* Various studies show that 50 to 90 percent of work time is spent in some communication task.
- *Your success is based on communication.* Other studies verify that your career advancement is correlated with your ability to communicate well.
- *Communication is increasingly important today.* Recent trends, such as increased globalization, technology, and specialization, make persuasive communication more crucial than ever.

WHY THIS BOOK WAS WRITTEN

The thousands of participants in various business and professional speaking and writing courses I have taught want a brief summary of communication techniques. Many busy professionals have found other books on communication skills too long, insultingly remedial, or full of irrelevant information.

This book is appropriate for you if you want a guide that is short, professional, and readable.

- *Short.* The book summarizes results and models culled from thousands of pages of text and research. I have omitted bulky examples, cases, footnotes, and exercises.
- *Professional.* This book includes only information that professionals will find useful. You will not find instructions for study skills, such as in-class writing and testing; secretarial skills, such as typing letters and answering telephones; artistic skills, such as writing dialogue and performing dramatic readings; or job-seeking skills, such as résumé writing and job interviewing.
- *Readable.* I have tried to make the book clear and practical. The format makes it easy to read and to skim. The tone is direct, matter-of-fact, and nontheoretical.

HOW THIS BOOK IS ORGANIZED

The book is divided into four main sections.

Communication strategy (Chapter I)

Effective managerial communication—written or oral—is based on an effective strategy. Therefore, you should analyze the five strategic variables covered in this chapter before you start to write or speak: (1) communicator strategy (objectives, style, and credibility); (2) audience strategy (who they are, what they know, what they feel, how you can motivate them); (3) message strategy (how to emphasize and organize); (4) channel choice strategy (when to write and when to speak); and (5) culture strategy (how cultural differences affect your strategy.)

Writing (Chapters II, III, IV, and appendices)

Chapter II offers techniques on the writing process, how to write more efficiently. Chapter III deals with "macro," or larger, issues in writing—including document design, structural signposts, and paragraphs or sections. Chapter IV covers "micro," or smaller, writing issues—including editing for brevity and choosing a style. The appendices cover writing formats, grammar, and punctuation.

Speaking (Chapters V, VI, and VII)

The speaking section discusses three aspects of business speaking. Chapter V explains the verbal aspects—or what you say—in presentations, question-and-answer sessions, interactive meetings, and other speaking situations. Chapter VI describes visual aids, both those prepared in advanced and those generated during the discussion. Chapter VII analyzes nonverbal delivery and listening skills.

Reference

The last section of the book contains appendices that deal with formats, unbiased language, grammar, and punctuation. Finally, the bibliography lists my sources. Refer to the bibliography for documentation or for further information about any ideas throughout the book.

ACKNOWLEDGMENTS

I offer grateful acknowledgment to the many people who helped make this book possible. First of all, my collegial family and my family of colleagues helped with ideas and revisions: Paul Argenti, Susan Eisner, Seth Daniel Munter, Lindsay Rahmun, Jay Rice, Lynn Russell, Susan Schwarz, Craig Snow, Greg Wadlinger, Kim Wardwell, and JoAnne Yates. Over the past twenty years, I have been privileged to work with excellent colleagues, executives, and students. My thanks to colleagues from the Managerial Communication Association and the Association for Business Communication for their research, energy, and stimulation. Thanks also to the thousands of executives from over eighty companies for their "real-world" experience and insights. I can scarcely believe that I have now taught literally thousands of students—at Dartmouth's Amos Tuck School of Business, Stanford Graduate School of Business, the International University of Japan, and the Helsinki School of Economics. To them, I offer my thanks for their challenges and ideas. Finally, I would like to acknowledge my sources listed in the bibliography.

Mary Munter
Amos Tuck School of Business
Dartmouth College

CHAPTER I OUTLINE

I. Communicator strategy
   1. What are your objectives?
   2. What communication style do you choose?
   3. What is your credibility?

II. Audience strategy
   1. Who are they?
   2. What do they know?
   3. What do they feel?
   4. How can you motivate them?

III. Message strategy
   1. How can you emphasize?
   2. How can you organize?

IV. Channel choice strategy

V. Culture strategy

CHAPTER 1

Communication Strategy

Managerial communication is different from other kinds of communication. Why? Because in a business or management setting, a brilliant message alone is not sufficient: you are successful only if your message leads to the response you desire from your audience. Therefore, instead of visualizing communication as a straight line from a sender to a receiver, think of communication as a circle, as shown below, with the audience's response as one of its critical elements.

To get that desired audience response, you need to think strategically about your communication—before you start to write or speak. Strategic communication is based on five variables, which you can analyze in any order: communicator (the writer or speaker) strategy, audience strategy, message strategy, channel choice strategy, and cultural context strategy. Each of these variables affects the others. For example, your audience analysis affects your style, your channel choice may affect your message, and the cultural context may affect your channel choice.

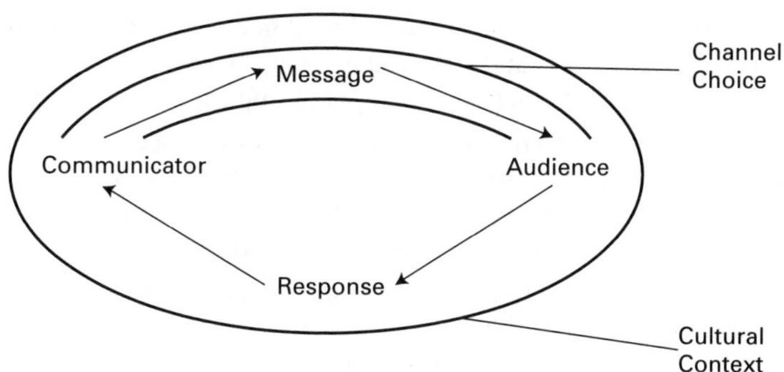

I. COMMUNICATOR STRATEGY

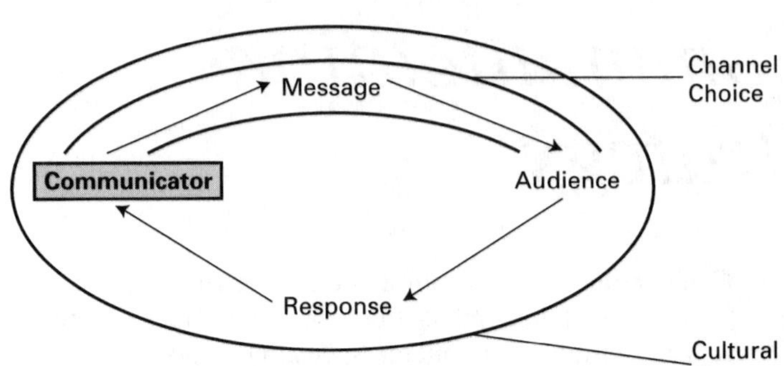

One element of your communication strategy has to do with a set of issues involving yourself, the person who is communicating. Regardless of whether you are speaking or writing, your communicator strategy includes defining your objectives, choosing a style, and enhancing your credibility.

1. What are your objectives?

Defining your objectives provides two important benefits. First, you will be more efficient, because you will no longer waste time writing or presenting material unless you have a clear reason for doing so. Second, you will be more effective, because formulating your objective precisely will help you communicate more clearly. To clarify your purpose, hone your objectives from the general to the specific.

General objectives These are your broad goals, the ones that trigger the creative process and start you thinking. They are comprehensive statements about what you hope to accomplish.

Action objectives To define your objectives more specifically, determine your action objectives—specific, measurable, time-bound steps that will lead toward your general objectives. State your action objectives in this form: "To accomplish a specific result by a specific time."

Communication objective Your communication objective is even more specific. Based on your action objectives, decide precisely how you hope your audience will respond to your written or oral communication. To define your communication objective, complete this statement: "As a result of this communication, my audience will . . ."

EXAMPLES OF OBJECTIVES		
General	**Action**	**Communication**
Communicate departmental results.	Report X times per X time period.	As a result of this presentation, my boss will learn what my department accomplished this month.
Increase customer base.	Contract with X number of clients per X time period.	As a result of this letter, the client will sign the contract.
Develop a sound financial position.	Maintain annual debt-to-equity ratio no greater than X.	As a result of this email, the accountant will give me the pertinent information for my report. As a result of this report, the board will approve my recommendations.
Increase the number of women hired.	Hire X number by X date.	As a result of this meeting, we will come up with a strategy to accomplish our goal. As a result of this presentation, at least X number of women will sign up to interview with my firm.
Maintain market share.	Sell X amount by X date.	As a result of this memo, my boss will approve my marketing plan. As a result of this presentation, the sales representatives will understand our product enhancements.

2. What communication style do you choose?

Once you have defined your communication objective, choose the appropriate style to accomplish that objective. The following framework, adapted from Tannenbaum and Schmidt, displays the range of communication styles used in virtually everyone's job at various times. Instead of trying to find one "right" style, use the appropriate style at the appropriate time and avoid using the same style all of the time.

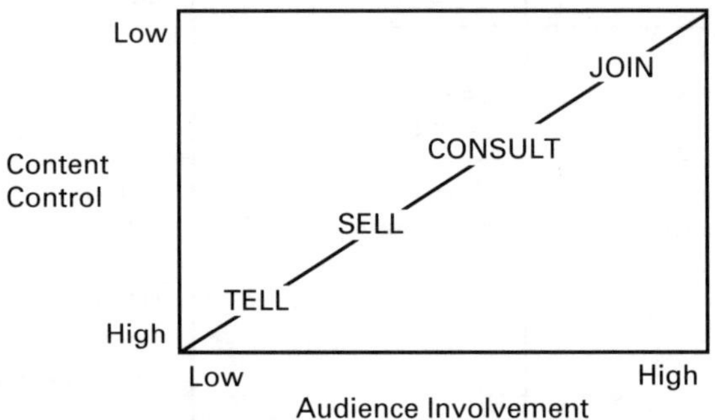

When to use the tell/sell style For the tell/sell style, you want your audience to learn from you. In the *tell* style, you are informing or explaining; you want your audience to understand something you already know. In the *sell* style, you are persuading or advocating; you want your audience to do something different. In tell/sell situations:

- You have sufficient information
- You do not need to hear others' opinions, ideas, or inputs
- You need to or want to control the message content yourself

When to use the consult/join style For the consult/join style, sometimes called the "inquiry style," you want to learn from the audience. The *consult* style is somewhat collaborative (like a questionnaire); the *join* style is even more collaborative (like a brainstorming session). In consult/join situations:

- You do not have sufficient information
- You need to or want to understand others' opinions, ideas, or inputs
- You need to or want to involve your audience, coming up with message content together

EXAMPLES OF OBJECTIVES AND STYLES	
Communication Objective	**Communication Style**
As a result of reading this memo, the employees will understand the benefits program available in this company. As a result of this presentation, my boss will learn what my department has accomplished this month.	**TELL:** In these situations, you are instructing or explaining. You want your audience to learn, to understand. You do not need your audience's opinions.
As a result of reading this letter, my client will sign the enclosed contract. As a result of this presentation, the committee will approve my proposed budget.	**SELL:** In these situations, you are persuading or advocating. You want your audience to do something different. You need some audience involvement to get them to do so.
As a result of reading this survey, the employees will respond by answering the questionnaire. As a result of this question-and-answer session, my staff will voice and obtain replies to their concerns about the new policy.	**CONSULT:** In these situations, you are conferring. You need some give-and-take with your audience. You want to learn from them, yet control the interaction somewhat.
As a result of reading this agenda memo, the group will come to the meeting prepared to offer their thoughts on this issue. As a result of this brainstorming session, the group will come up with a solution to this problem.	**JOIN:** In these situations, you are collaborating. You and your audience are working together to come up with the content.

3. What is your credibility?

Another aspect of communicator strategy involves analyzing your audience's perception of you. In other words, consider your own credibility: their belief, confidence, and faith in you. Their perception of you has a tremendous impact on how you should communicate with them.

Five factors (based on social power theorists French, Raven, and Kotter) affect your credibility: (1) rank, (2) goodwill, (3) expertise, (4) image, and (5) common ground. Once you understand these factors, you can enhance your credibility by stressing your initial credibility and by increasing your acquired credibility.

Initial credibility Initial credibility refers to your audience's perception of you before you even begin to communicate, before they ever read or hear what you have to say. Your initial credibility, then, may stem from their perception of who you are, what you represent, or how you have related to them previously.

As part of your communication strategy, you may want to stress or remind your audience of your initial credibility. Also, in those lucky situations in which your initial credibility is high, you may use it as a "bank account." If people in your audience regard you highly, they may trust you even in unpopular or extreme decisions or recommendations. Just as drawing on a bank account reduces your bank balance, however, drawing on your initial credibility reduces your credibility balance; you must "deposit" more to your account, perhaps by goodwill gestures or further proof of your expertise.

Acquired credibility In contrast, acquired credibility refers to your audience's perception of you after the communication has taken place, after they have read or heard what you have to say. Even if your audience knows nothing about you in advance, your good ideas and your persuasive writing or speaking will help earn you credibility. The obvious way to heighten your credibility, therefore, is to do a good job of analyzing and communicating in general.

In addition, consider choosing from among the techniques listed on the chart on the facing page.

FACTORS AND TECHNIQUES FOR CREDIBILITY			
Factor	**Based on...**	**Stress initial credibility by...**	**Increase acquired credibility by...**
Rank	Hierarchical power	Emphasizing your title or rank	Associating yourself with or citing a high-ranking person (e.g., by his or her cover letter or introduction)
Goodwill	Personal relationship or "track record"	Referring to relationship or "track record"	Building your goodwill by emphasizing audience benefits, "what's in it for them"
	Trustworthiness	Offering balanced evaluation; acknowledging any conflict of interest	
Expertise	Knowledge, competence	Sharing your expert understanding Explaining how you gained your expertise	Associating yourself with or citing authoritative sources
Image	Attractiveness, audience desire to be like you	Emphasizing attributes audience finds attractive	Building your image by identifying yourself with your audience's benefits; using nonverbals and language your audience considers dynamic
Common ground	Common values, ideas, problems, or needs	Establishing your shared values or ideas Acknowledging similarities with audience Tying the message to your common ground	

II. AUDIENCE STRATEGY

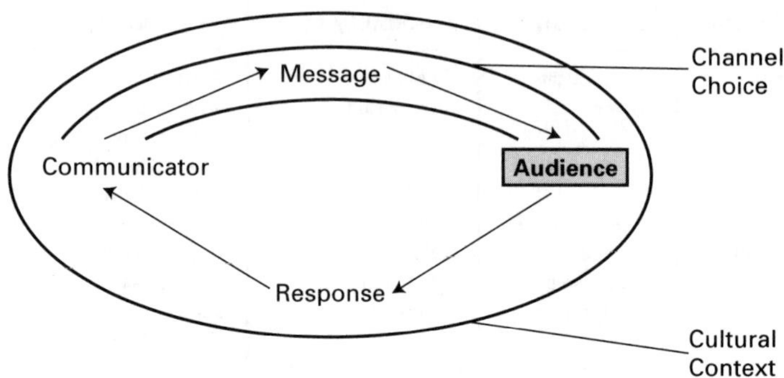

Audience strategy—that is, techniques for gearing your communication toward your audience's needs and interests—is possibly the most important aspect of your communication strategy, because it has the most effect on increasing your chances of being understood and of achieving your objective. Some communication experts recommend performing your audience analysis first; others recommend performing your communicator strategy first. All experts agree, however, that the two strategies interact with and affect one another. So, perhaps the best idea is to perform these analyses concurrently.

Audience strategy includes answering four sets of questions: (1) Who are they? (2) What do they know? (3) What do they feel? (4) How can you motivate them?

1. Who are they?

"Who are they?" sounds like a fairly straightforward question, yet choosing the people to include and focus on is often subtle and complex. To decide whom to include and how to analyze them, answer these two sets of questions.

Who should be included in your audience? In many business situations, you have, or might consider having, multiple audiences. If you are writing or speaking to more than one person, gear your message toward the person or people with the most influence over accomplishing your communication objective.

- *Primary:* First of all, decide who will be included in your primary audience—those who will receive your written or spoken message directly.
- *Secondary:* Consider any secondary or "hidden" audiences—such as those who will receive a copy of, need to approve, hear about, or be affected by your message.
- *Gatekeeper:* Is there a "gatekeeper" in your audience—someone you will need to route the message? If so, is there any reason he or she might block your message?
- *Opinion leader:* Is there anyone in the audience who has significant informal influence?
- *Key decision maker:* Finally, and perhaps most importantly, is there a key decision maker, with power on or influence over the outcome of the communication? If so, gear your message toward her or him.

How can you find out about them? Once you have figured out who is or should be in your audience, analyze them as carefully as possible. Sometimes you may have market research or other data available. But most of the time, audience analysis is more subjective—asking the advice of someone you trust, reflecting on your past impressions, or empathizing with or imagining you are your audience.

- *As individuals:* If you can, analyze each audience member individually. Think about their educational level, training, age, sex, and interests. What are their opinions, interests, expectations, and attitudes?
- *As a group:* Even if you don't know them individually, you can analyze them as a group. What are their group characteristics? What does the group stand for? What are their shared norms, traditions, standards, rules, and values?

2. What do they know?

Based on your audience analysis, think about what they know and what they need to know. More specifically, ask yourself these three sets of questions.

How much background information do they need? What do they already know about the topic? How much jargon will they understand?

- *Low background needs:* If their background information needs are low, don't waste their time with unnecessary background or definitions.
- *High background needs:* If their background information needs are high, be sure to define new terms or jargon, link new information to information they already know, and use extremely clear structure.
- *Mixed background needs:* With mixed audiences, try including background information with an opening such as "just to review," or putting background information in a separate appendix or handout.

How much new information do they need? What do they need to learn about the topic? How much detail and evidence do they need?

- *High information needs:* If they need it, provide sufficient evidence, statistics, data, and other material. Do they need the sources documented? If so, are the sources credible to them?
- *Low information needs:* On the other hand, many times they don't need a lot of new information: for example, they may trust your expert opinion or delegate the decision to you. Think in terms of how much information your audience needs, not how much information you can possibly provide.
- *Mixed information needs:* With mixed audiences, try including additional detail in a separate appendix or handout.

What are their expectations and preferences? What do they expect or prefer in terms of style, channel, or format?

- *Style preferences:* What, if anything, do they expect in terms of cultural, organizational, or personal style—such as formal or informal, straightforward or indirect, interactive or noninteractive?
- *Channel preferences:* What, if anything, do they expect in terms of channel choice—such as hard copy versus email or group versus individual meetings?
- *Standard length and format preferences:* What, if anything, do they expect in terms of standard document or presentation length or format—such as a standard format for one-page memos or standard half-hour weekly informal meetings?

3. What do they feel?

Remember, your audience's emotional level is just as important as their knowledge level. Therefore, in addition to thinking about what they know, think about what they feel. Answering the following sets of questions will give you a sense of the emotions your audience may be bringing to the communication.

What emotions do they feel? What feelings may arise from their current situation or their emotional attitude?

- *What is their current situation?* Is there anything about the economic situation, the timing, or their morale that you should keep in mind?
- *What emotions might they feel about your message?* Many communicators mistakenly think that all business audiences are driven by facts and rationality alone. In truth, they may also be driven by their feelings about your message: they may feel positive emotions such as pride, excitement, and hope, or negative emotions, such as anxiety, fear, or jealousy.

How interested are they in your message? Is your message a high priority or low priority for your audience? How likely are they to choose to read what you write or to listen carefully to what you say? How curious are they and how much do they care about the issue or its outcomes?

- *High interest level:* If their interest level is high, you can get right to the point without taking much time to arouse their interest. Build a good logical argument. Do not expect a change of opinion without continued effort over time; however, if you can persuade them, their change will be more permanent than changes in a low-interest audience.
- *Low interest level:* If, on the other hand, their interest level is low, think about using a consult/join style and ask them to participate: one of the strongest ways to build support is to share control. If, however, you are using a tell/sell style, use one or more of the techniques discussed on pages 15–17 to motivate their interest. In addition, keep your message as short as possible; long documents are intimidating and listeners tune out what seems like rambling. Finally, for low-interest audiences, act quickly on attitude changes because they may not be permanent.

What is their probable bias: positive or negative? What is their probable attitude toward your ideas or recommendations? Are they likely to favor them, be indifferent, or be opposed? What do they have to gain or lose from your ideas? Why might they say "no"?

- *Positive or neutral:* If they are positive or neutral, reinforce their existing attitude by stating the benefits that will accrue from your message.
- *Negative:* If they are negative, try one or more of these techniques: (1) Get them to agree that there is a problem, then solve the problem. (2) State points with which you think they will agree first; if audience members are sold on two or three key features of your proposal, they will tend to sell themselves on the other features as well. (3) Limit your request to the smallest one possible, such as a pilot program rather than a full program right away. (4) Respond to anticipated objections; you will be more persuasive by stating and rejecting alternatives than having them devise their own, which they will be less likely to reject.

Is your desired action easy or hard for them? From their perspective, what will your communication objective entail in terms of their immediate task? Will it be time-consuming, complicated, or difficult for them?

- *Easy or hard for them:* Whether your desired action is easy or hard, always show how it supports their beliefs or benefits.
- *Hard for them:* If it is hard, try one of these techniques: (1) Break the action down into the smallest possible request, such as a signature approving an idea for someone else lined up to implement it. (2) Make the action as easy as you can, such as distributing a questionnaire that they can fill in easily or providing them with a checklist they can follow easily.

4. How can you motivate them?

Of the following three sets of motivational techniques, choose those that will work best for your particular audience.

Can you motivate through audience benefits? Stress "what's in it for them."

- *Tangible benefits:* What tangible benefits, if any, can you offer your audience? Emphasize their value (e.g., profits, savings, bonuses, or product discounts) or significance as symbols (e.g., offices, furnishings, or jewelry). Effective tangible benefits do not need to be elegant. Items such as T-shirts, mugs, or pens will work effectively—if they are valued by the audience.
- *Career or task benefits:* (1) Sometimes you can motivate by showing how your message will enhance your audience's job—by solving a current problem, saving them time, or making their job easier or more convenient. (2) Or you can appeal to the task itself. Some audiences may appreciate the chance to be challenged, or to participate in tough problem solving or decision making. (3) Other people respond to appeals to their career advancement or prestige. Let them know how they will win organizational recognition and visibility, or enhance their reputation or networking contacts.
- *Ego benefits:* Some people respond to motivational devices that enhance their sense of self-worth, accomplishment, and achievement. For example, show them they are accepted and included by soliciting their suggestions or inviting them to participate. You can incorporate emotional support into your communication with informal verbal praise or with nonverbal smiles and nods with more formal statements.
- *Group benefits:* For audiences who value group relationships and group identity, emphasize benefits to the group as a whole: appeal to any tangible group benefits, group task enhancements, group advancements, or sense of group worth. For audiences who value solidarity with the group, use statements of group consensus or coalition rather than expert testimony or your individual credibility. For people who are very strongly influenced by the beliefs and actions of those around them, use the "bandwagon" technique. In the words of communication expert JoAnne Yates, "Although the fact that 'everyone is doing it' may not be a very good logical argument, it nevertheless influences some people."

Can you motivate through credibility? On pages 8–9, we discussed various factors that influence your credibility. Here are some techniques to apply your credibility as a motivational tool. Remember, the less your audience is involved in the topic or issue, the more important your credibility is as a motivating factor.

- *Shared value credibility and the "common ground" technique:* One of the strongest applications of shared value credibility is to establish a "common ground" with your audience, especially at the beginning of your message. If you initially express opinions held in common with your audience, you will be more likely to change their opinions on other issues. Therefore, by starting from a common ground, even on an unrelated subject, you can increase your chance of persuading them of your main point. For example, refer to goals you share with your audience before focusing on your disagreement over how to achieve them.
- *Goodwill credibility and the "reciprocity" technique:* A motivational technique applying goodwill credibility is called "reciprocity" or "bargaining." People generally feel obligated to reciprocate positive actions with other positive actions and concessions with concessions. So, you might gain a favor by granting a favor; you might offer a concession to gain a concession. People feel obliged to reciprocate gifts, favors, and concessions—even uninvited or unwanted ones.
- *Rank credibility and punishment techniques:* The most extreme application of rank credibility is using threats and punishments, such as reprimands, pay cuts, demotions, or even dismissal. Although managers must use threats and punishments in certain situations, you should do so with extreme caution. Researchers have found that threats produce tension, provoke counteraggression, increase fear and dislike, work only when you're on the spot to assure compliance, and may eliminate an undesired behavior without producing the desired behavior. Therefore, threats and punishments are inappropriate for most audiences and most situations.

Can you motivate through message structure? Finally, in some situations, you might motivate your audience by the way you structure your message.

- *Opening:* Arouse their interest in the opening, especially if it is low, by (1) emphasizing "what's in it for them," (2) convincing them there's a problem that needs solving, or (3) explaining how the message relates to them, especially if that relationship is not immediately apparent.
- *Body of the message:* In some situations, what you say in the body of the message can enhance your persuasiveness. (1) *The two-sided technique:* If your audience's attitude is negative, or you believe they will hear opposing arguments, present both sides of the question. The more strongly your audience is likely to object, the sooner you should deal with their objections. They will not hear your positive arguments until their concerns have been addressed. This technique works because you appear more reasonable and fair-minded, and because people are more likely to reject alternatives explained to them than alternatives they think up themselves. (2) *The "foot in the door" technique:* Break the action down into the smallest possible request, one that you are likely to get (such as a pilot program), then later you will be more likely to get the larger request. Alternatively, get someone to commit to a position publicly—even if he or she does not believe in it strongly. People will often become stronger supporters once they have made a public commitment. (3) *The "door in the face" technique:* The opposite of the "foot in the door" technique, the "door in the face" technique involves making an extreme request that you fully expect to be rejected, followed by a more moderate request that is then more likely to be honored. (4) *The "inoculation" technique:* "Inoculate" them with a mild opposing view, then "cure" them by refution. Thus, you protect them from future infection.
- *Ending:* The message ending is another place you might use motivational techniques. (1) Make it easy for your audience to act: for example, use a questionnaire they can fill in easily or a checklist they can follow easily; or list specific next steps or specific actions. (2) Once again, emphasize "what's in it for them" at the end of your message.

III. MESSAGE STRATEGY

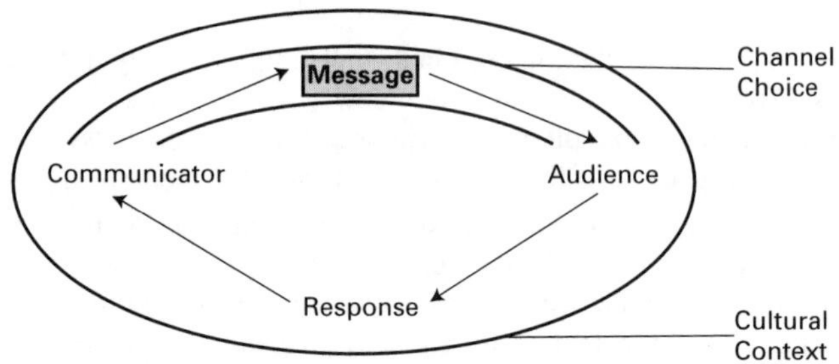

Structuring your message is a third variable in your communication strategy. Ineffective communicators simply state their ideas in the order they happen to occur to them; effective communicators think strategically about how best to structure their message. When you think, all kinds of ideas occur to you—some good, some bad, some complete, some fragmented; the end result of the thought process is your conclusion. But you don't want your audience to have to wade through all the false starts and disjointed ideas you went through during the thought process, so when you communicate strategically you emphasize and organize your ideas clearly for your audience. The following illustration graphically demonstrates this difference:

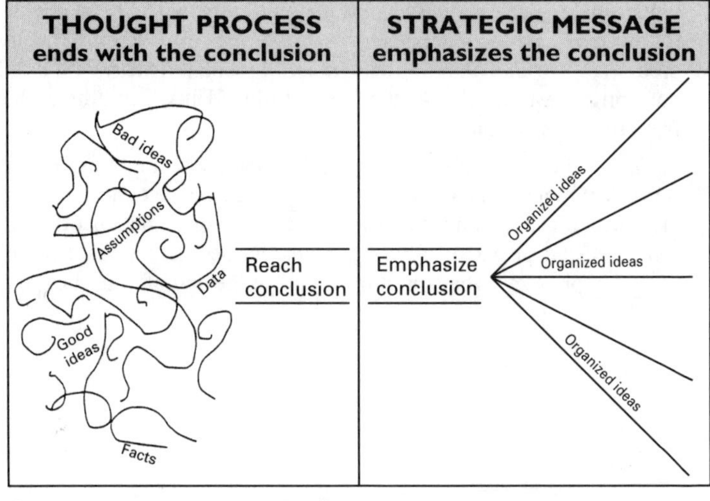

Instead of structuring your message as ideas happen to occur to you, ask yourself the following questions: (1) How can you emphasize? (2) How can you organize?

1. How can you emphasize?

The Audience Memory Curve, illustrated below, summarizes research on what your audience is most likely to remember from your message.

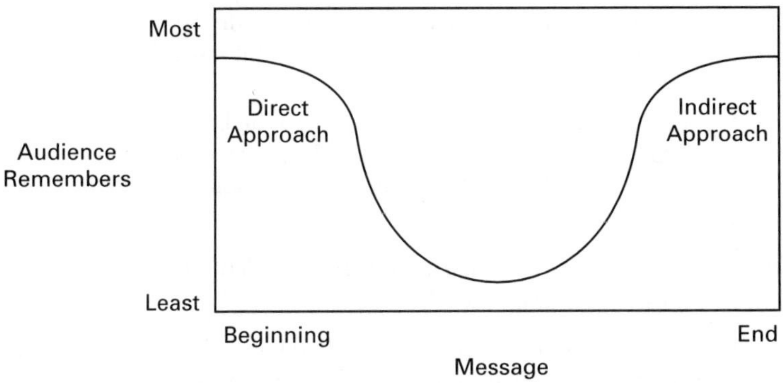

What does the Audience Memory Curve imply? First, that you should never bury important ideas in the middle. Second, that you need to keep your audience's attention throughout by using the audience motivational appeals described on pages 15–17. Third, that your opening or introduction is extremely important. Finally, that you should state your important ideas prominently—either at the beginning or at the end (or both).

Stating your main ideas first is called the direct approach; stating them last is called the indirect approach.

Using the direct approach The direct approach, stating your main ideas at the beginning of the Audience Memory Curve, is sometimes called "bottom-lining" your message, because you state the bottom line first. For example,

> The committee recommends policy x for the following reasons:
>
> Reason 1
>
> Reason 2
>
> Reason 3

Advantages of the direct approach Using the direct approach has many advantages.

- *Improves comprehension:* People assimilate and comprehend content more easily when they know the conclusions first. Withholding your conclusion until the end is fine for a mystery story, but not for a busy business audience who may resent every minute they spend trying to figure out what you're getting at.
- *Is audience centered:* The direct approach emphasizes the results of your analysis—unlike the indirect approach, which is communicator centered because it mirrors the steps you went through to formulate your conclusions.
- *Saves time:* The direct approach saves your audience time. They can understand the message with little rereading or repetition, and they can decide immediately which sections they can skim, read carefully, or use as reference.

Why the direct approach is underutilized Why, then, do people often avoid the direct approach?

- *Habit:* For one thing, communicators find it is easier to write or speak the way they think, even though it is harder on their readers or listeners.
- *Academic training:* Many communicators have been reinforced in the use of indirect structure throughout years of schooling.
- *Suspense:* Some communicators think the indirect strategy will build suspense and keep their audience's attention. In fact, however, it merely befuddles them.
- *Effort:* Finally, some people want their audience to appreciate all the effort they went through, when, in fact, such an approach may lead to unnecessary confusion rather than understanding.

When to use the direct approach Because the direct approach is easier and faster to follow, you should use it as much as possible in Anglo-American business situations, probably about 90% of the time. (See pages 29–31 for more on cultural differences.) Specifically, use the direct approach for:

- All nonsensitive messages, that is, those with no emotional overtones
- Sensitive messages if the audience's bias is positive
- Sensitive messages if the audience is results oriented
- Sensitive messages if your credibility is particularly high.

Using the indirect approach An indirect approach, saving your main idea until the end of the Audience Memory Curve, involves spelling out your support first, then finishing with your generalization or conclusion. Indirect structure is sometimes called the "mystery story approach." For example,

Reason 1

Reason 2

Reason 3

Therefore, the committee recommends policy x.

When to use the indirect approach Because this approach is harder for and takes longer for your audience to understand, and because it does not take advantage of the audience's attentiveness at the beginning of the message, use it only when all four of the following conditions apply:

- Sensitive message (with emotional overtones) *and*
- Your audience's bias is negative *and*
- Your audience is analysis oriented *and*
- Your credibility is low.

Advantages of the indirect approach In the situation in which all four of these conditions apply, the indirect strategy may soften your audience's resistance, arouse their interest, and increase their tendency to see you as fair-minded. Also, the indirect approach gives you the chance to let your audience "buy into" ideas they agree with or a problem they need to solve, before you present your solution.

2. How can you organize?

Once you have emphasized your main idea by placing it first (direct approach) or last (indirect approach), organize your supporting points accordingly.

EXAMPLES OF STRATEGIC MESSAGES			
Communication objective	**If it is a…**	**Then, use this approach…**	**And organize by…**
Staff will follow procedure	Routine procedure	Direct	Listing the steps in the procedure
	New procedure, hostile audience	Indirect	Discussing the benefits of procedure, followed by steps in procedure
Boss will approve plan	Busy audience, or your credibility high	Direct	Explaining the plan, then the reasons why
	Analytic audience, and your credibility low	Indirect	List the supporting reasons, then the plan
Customer will purchase our service	Audience is results oriented, or bias is indifferent	Direct	Recommending your service, followed by audience benefits from service
	Audience bias is negative	Indirect	Listing the benefits from your service and/or problems with competitor's service, then recommend your service

IV. CHANNEL CHOICE STRATEGY

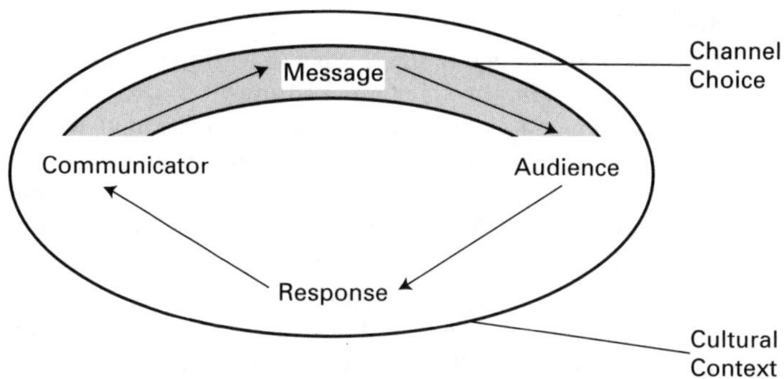

Channel choice refers to the choice of medium through which you send your message. In the past, this strategic choice was basically between two channels: writing and speaking. Many more channels exist today—including fax, email, voicemail, electronic meetings, and videoteleconferencing; these new channels sometimes change the nature of how we traditionally thought about channel choice. For example, traditional writing is usually fairly reserved and controlled; email, however, may be less reserved and controlled.

Before you choose a channel from among this expanded set of alternatives, think about these general questions. Do you need to (1) *be formal or informal*? Both writing and speaking can be either formal or informal (e.g., formal reports or informal emails, formal presentations or informal meetings); (2) *receive an immediate response* and control over message being received or not? (3) *elicit high audience participation or not*? face-to face or not? (4) *have a "rich" communication or not*? Text only is the least rich channel; text plus pictures plus voice plus body language is the most rich channel. (5) *have a permanent record or not*? retransmit easily or not? (6) *use a channel preferred by your audience* or their culture?

Once you have considered these general issues, choose from among the following options, weighing the advantages and disadvantages of each. If you do not have your choice of channels, think about how you can utilize the advantages of, and overcome the disadvantages of, the channel you need to use.

1. Writing

Writing channels include traditional writing, fax, email, and web page.

Traditional writing

- *Advantages of traditional writing:* Choose writing when you want to (1) use precise wording and grammar, because you can edit, (2) include a great deal of detail, because readers can assimilate more detail than listeners, (3) save time for your audience, because reading is faster than listening, (4) have a private communication, (5) reach a geographically dispersed audience, (6) have a permanent and accessible record.
- *Disadvantages of traditional writing:* If you write, you will have (1) delayed transmission time, (2) no control over if or when the message is received, (3) a delayed response, if any, (4) no nonverbal communication, (5) possible lack of flexibility and too much rigidity.

Facsimile (fax)

- *Advantages:* Same as traditional writing, but with faster transmission time and can "blast fax" to multiple audiences simultaneously.
- *Disadvantages:* Same as traditional writing, but usually less private and may not reproduce graphics precisely.

Electronic mail (email)

- *Advantages:* Same as traditional writing, plus (1) less likely to be inhibited and reserved, at best, more likely to be spontaneous and creative, (2) less likely to take much preparation time, (3) more likely to contact people in all levels of an organization, (4) more likely to include written nonverbal cues by using "emoticons," such as : -) : - (, (5) easy for audience to respond quickly, (6) can "blast email" to multiple audiences simultaneously.
- *Disadvantages:* (1) May be inappropriately uninhibited or irresponsible, at worst, destructive (known as "flaming"); (2) may be hard to read because less likely to edit, full of typos and mistakes, and, more importantly, lack of logical frameworks for the reader—such as headings and transitions; (3) may include email jargon the reader does not understand—such as BTW ("by the way") or LOL ("laughing out loud"); (4) cannot ever be erased or shredded, becomes property of the company, may be used in lawsuits; (5) may be sent to the wrong person by mistake and irretrievably, forwarded without your permission, sent to too many people unnecessarily; (6) may be a way to avoid confrontation or to avoid consensus building; (7) may be responded to too quickly or mistaken for formal text or formal commitment.

Web page

- *Advantages:* (1) Provides easy access to document at all times, (2) can reach audiences you don't know.
- *Disadvantages:* (1) Least personal and private written channel, (2) usually one-way communication, (3) not addressed to specific audience; they have to look for it.

2. Speaking to a group (face to face)

You can speak to a group in a tell/sell or a consult/join style.

Tell/sell presentations

- *Advantages:* Compared to writing, choose presentations when you want to (1) control if and when the message is received and have your audience hear the same information at the same time, (2) receive an immediate and interactive response, (3) include nonverbal communication, (4) build group identity and group relationships. Compared to meetings, choose presentations when you want to (1) use the tell or sell styles, (2) speak yourself most of the time.
- *Disadvantages:* Presentations (1) are less private and confidential than writing, (2) do not provide a permanent and accessible record, (3) require that audience must be in the same place, (4) do not allow as much detail as writing, because listeners cannot assimilate as much detail as readers, (5) are less precise than writing, because you cannot edit what you say, (6) may be intimidating and dominated by the speaker.

Consult/join meetings

- *Advantages:* Compared to presentations, choose meetings when you want to (1) elicit ideas from others, (2) foster group participation and discussion, (3) resolve group issues, (4) receive input from various people or groups, (5) reach a consensus and establish action steps, (6) use consult or join styles. Compared to electronic meetings, choose face-to-face meetings when (1) you need the richest nonverbal cues, including body, voice, proximity, and touch; (2) the issues are especially sensitive; (3) the people don't know one another; (4) establishing group rapport and relationships is crucial.
- *Disadvantages:* Compared to videoconferences, face-to-face meetings (1) do not allow the possibility of simultaneous participation by people in multiple locations, (2) can delay meeting follow-up activities because decisions and action items must be written up after the meeting. Compared to electronic meetings, face-to-face meetings may be dominated by overly vocal, quick-to-speak, and higher-status participants; may involve high travel costs and time.

3. Speaking to a group (electronically)

Unlike the face-to-face speaking channels discussed previously, the following three channels use different kinds of *groupware*—a broad term for a group of related technologies that mediate group collaboration through technology—that may include any combination of collaborative software or intraware, electronic- and voice-mail systems, electronic meeting systems, phone systems, video systems, electronic bulletin boards, and group document handling and annotation systems.

Videoconferences

- *Advantages:* Choose videoconferences when (1) the participants are in different places, but you want to communicate with them all at the same time, (2) you want to save on travel time and expenses, (3) you want to inform, explain, or train—as opposed to persuade or sell, (4) you want to record a video for reuse.
- *Disadvantages:* (1) They are usually not as effective as face-to-face meetings when you need to persuade or to establish personal relationships; (2) they lack the richest nonverbal cues, such as proximity and touch; (3) fewer people tend to speak and they speak in longer bursts than in other kinds of meetings; (4) they may involve significant set-up time and costs.

Broadcasting or webcasting

- *Advantages:* Can transmit to multiple audiences in multiple locations.
- *Disadvantages:* Usually one-way video, sometimes two-way audio.

Electronic meetings Electronic meeting systems (EMS)—with participants writing on their computers—are *mediated* (that is, they utilize a trained technical facilitator) and usually *synchronous* (that is, everyone participates at the same time).

- *Advantages of EMS:* Choose electronic meetings when you want to (1) generate more ideas and alternatives more quickly than with a traditional note-taker; (2) allow the possibility of anonymous input, which may lead to more candid and truthful replies, equalize participants' status, and increase participation among hierarchical levels; (3) maximize audience participation and in-depth discussion because everyone can "speak" simultaneously, so shy members are more likely to participate and the "vocal few" are less likely to dominate the discussion; (4) provide immediate documentation when meeting is finished.

- *Disadvantages of EMS:* EMS (1) cannot replace face-to-face contact, especially when group efforts are just beginning and when you are trying to build group values, trust, and emotional ties, (2) may exacerbate dysfunctional group dynamics and increased honesty may lead to increased conflict; (3) may make it harder to reach consensus, because more ideas are generated and because it may be harder to interpret the strength of other members' commitment to their proposals; (4) may demand a good deal of facilitator preparation time and training.

Email meetings Email meetings are *unmediated* (that is, messages go directly to other participants' computers) and *asynchronous* (that is, people respond at their convenience, at different times).

- *Advantages:* At their best, email meetings can (1) increase participation because people can respond when they wish and no scheduling is necessary; (2) speed up meeting follow-up activities because of electronic distribution; (3) decrease transmission time for circulating documents; (4) allow quick discussion and resolution of many small or obscure issues or problems; (5) decrease writing inhibitions with more conversational style than traditional writing; (6) increase communication across hierarchical boundaries.
- *Disadvantages:* At their worst, email meetings can (1) decrease attention to the audience and to social context and regulation; (2) be inappropriately uninhibited or irresponsible, at worst destructive (known as "flaming"); (3) be inappropriately informal; (4) consist of "quick and dirty" messages, with typos and grammatical errors, and, more importantly, lack of logical frameworks for readers—such as headings and transitions; (5) result in a delayed response, or no response; (6) make it harder to gain commitment than with other kinds of meetings.

Conference calls Conference calls are group calls by telephone.

- *Advantages:* Same as videoconferencing, plus allow for quicker response with less set-up time and use more easily accessible equipment.
- *Disadvantages:* Same as videoconferencing, but lack of body language makes it harder to interact and to know who is going to speak next, and lack of text or visuals makes it harder to communicate a great deal of detailed information.

4. Speaking to an individual

Speak to an individual—not to a group—when you want (1) a private, confidential communication, (2) individual feedback or response, (3) less preparation time, or (4) a fast, simple answer.

Conversation (face-to-face)

- *Advantages:* Compared to email or voicemail, talk with someone face-to-face when (1) you want to build your individual relationship or rapport, (2) the message is especially sensitive or negative, (3) you want a candid, low-risk, fast reply.
- *Disadvantages:* Lacks most of the advantages of writing and speaking to a group, plus (1) the person must be located in the same place as you are, (2) if you speak with more than one person, they will hear different information at different times, (3) may be easily misunderstood with no permanent record, (4) may make some people feel excluded.

Telephone

- *Advantages:* (1) Good for candid, low-risk, fast replies, (2) better than face-to-face for reaching people in different places, saves time and travel costs, (3) better than voicemail for establishing rapport.
- *Disadvantages:* (1) Harder to build a personal relationship because fewer nonverbal cues than one-to-one, (2) if you telephone more than one person, they will hear different information at different times.

Voicemail

- *Advantages:* Use voicemail when you want (1) to handle small items quickly; (2) faster distribution than with paper; (3) more emotional content than email, because of nonverbal vocal cues; (4) messages more easily retrieved than email, no computer required; (5) to "blast voicemail" to multiple audiences simultaneously; (6) less likelihood of permanent record being made, (7) to forward others' vocal messages with your comments.
- *Disadvantages:* (1) Like writing, when you use voicemail, you will have a delayed response, no control over if and when message is received, and no immediate interactivity; (2) like email, voicemail may be forwarded on and distributed widely without your permission; (3) lacks a record; (4) is usually effective for brief messages only; (5) may carry less weight than a document: people may listen to the first part and delete or skip over entirely.

V. CULTURE STRATEGY

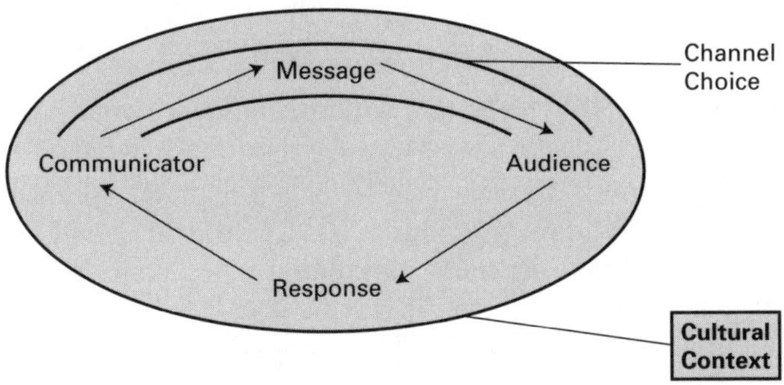

Every aspect of communication strategy we have discussed so far will be greatly influenced by the cultural context in which you are communicating. These cultural differences could result from different countries, regions, industries, organizations, genders, ethnic groups, or work groups. The danger in cultural analysis is stereotyping: saying all the people in a group behave a certain way all of the time, usually phrased negatively, such as "all British people are cold." A more useful approach is to think in terms of cultural norms: saying most people in a group behave a certain way most of the time, expressed as a behavior, not as a judgment, such as "the British tend to use formal greetings."

Communicator strategy The culture in which you communicate will affect all three aspects of communicator strategy.

Communication objective Rethink your communication objective in terms of the culture. (1) *Time:* Consider cultural attitudes toward time: you may want to set a different objective in a culture that is relative, relaxed, and tradition oriented about time than you would in a culture that is precise and future oriented toward time. (2) *Attitude:* Think also about the cultural attitude toward fate: the objective you set in a culture believing in deterministic fate may be different from one set in a culture believing in human control over fate.

Communication style Different communication styles will tend to work better in different cultures. Group-oriented cultures may favor consult/join styles; individualistic cultures may favor tell/sell styles. Autocratic cultures may favor tell styles; democratic cultures may favor consult styles.

Credibility Different cultures place different value on the five aspects of credibility. For instance, goodwill credibility is more important in cultures that value personal relations; expert credibility is more important in cultures that value hard facts and task orientation. Similarly, some cultures value rank, titles, and authority more than others.

Audience strategy The culture will also influence your audience strategy.

Audience selection You may need to include additional primary audiences (people who receive your message indirectly), and leaders (key decision makers), depending on cultural expectations about rank, authority, and group definition. Also, remember that different cultures have different attitudes toward age, sex, and educational level.

Audience motivation Different audience motivational techniques will work more effectively in different cultures. Although some cultures value material wealth and acquisition, others place greater value on work relationships, challenges, or status. Some cultures value Western logic more than others. The relative importance of individual relationships and credibility varies, as does the relative importance of group relationships and identity. Finally, values and ideals vary tremendously among cultures.

Gender-based tendencies Sometimes it's useful to think about the cultural differences between men and women. Research shows, for example, that men tend to take arguments impersonally, women personally; that men seek quick authoritative decisions, women use consensus building; that men use stronger language even when they're not sure, women use more qualified language even when they are sure; and that men use less active listening, women use more.

Message strategy In addition, cultural factors will influence your choice of message structure. Cultures valuing slow, ritualistic negotiations may favor indirect structure; cultures valuing fast, efficient negotiations may favor direct structures. Authoritarian cultures may favor direct structures downward and indirect structures upward.

Channel strategy Different cultures may have different norms for channel and form—for example, a technical department versus a marketing department or a traditional organization versus a start-up venture. These norms may range from standardized one-page memos to face-to-face hallway discussions. In addition, cultures valuing personal trust more than hard facts tend to prefer oral communication and oral agreements; cultures valuing facts and efficiency tend to prefer written communication and written agreements.

Nonverbal considerations In addition to the other strategic variables we have discussed in this chapter, nonverbal differences present another set of challenges in cross-cultural communication.

Body and voice Consider cultural norms regarding body and voice: posture, gestures, eye contact and direction of gaze, facial expression, touching behaviors, pitch, volume, rate, and attitude toward silence. Avoid gestures considered rude or insulting in that culture; resist applying your own culture's nonverbal meanings to other cultures. For example, Vietnamese may look down to show respect, but that doesn't mean they are "shifty." Northeasterners may speak fast, but that doesn't mean they are "arrogant."

Space and objects Also consider norms regarding space and objects: how much personal space people expect or need, how much institutional space people receive (who works where, with how much space, and with what material objects), how people dress, and how rigid dress codes are. For example, Latin Americans may prefer closer social space; Swedes may prefer more distant social space.

Greetings and hospitality Finally, consider cultural norms regarding greetings and hospitality: how people greet one another—handshakes, hugs, bows, and so forth—and expectations regarding food and hospitality—when, where, what, and how food is prepared, presented, and eaten. Knowing these norms can go a long way toward increasing your rapport and credibility.

Once you have set your communication strategy by analyzing all five variables covered in this chapter, then refer to the appropriate chapters:

- *For writing:* Turn to Chapters II, III, and IV, and appendices.
- *For speaking:* Turn to Chapters V, VI, and VII.

COMMUNICATION STRATEGY CHECKLIST

Communicator Strategy

See pages 4–9.

1. What is your communication objective: "As a result of this communication, my audience will . . . "?
2. What communication style do you choose: tell, sell, consult, or join?
3. What is your credibility: rank, goodwill, expertise, image, common ground?

Audience Strategy

See pages 10–17.

1. Who are they: primary, secondary, gatekeeper, opinion leader(s), key decision maker(s)?
2. How can you analyze them: as individuals? as a group?
3. What do they know: necessary background information and new information, expectations for style, channel, and format?
4. What do they feel: interest level, probable bias, hard or easy for them?

Message Strategy

See pages 18–22.

1. How can you emphasize: direct or indirect?
2. How can you organize a strategic message?

Channel Choice Strategy

See pages 23–28.

1. Writing: traditional, fax, email, or web page?
2. Speaking to a group face-to-face: tell/sell presentation or consult/join meeting?
3. Speaking to a group electronically: videoconference, broadcast or webcast, electronic meeting, email meeting, or conference call?
4. Speaking to an individual: face-to-face, telephone, or voicemail?

Culture Strategy

See pages 29–31.

1. How does the culture affect the communicator strategy: objective, style, credibility?
2. How does the culture affect the audience strategy: selection and motivation?
3. How does the culture affect the message strategy: direct or indirect?
4. How does the culture affect the channel choice strategy?
5. What nonverbal considerations should you keep in mind?

GUIDE TO THE GUIDE TO MANAGERIAL COMMUNICATION

To set your communication strategy → See Chapter I

- Communicator strategy (objectives, style, and credibility)
- Audience strategy (selection, analysis, and motivation)
- Message strategy (emphasis and organization)
- Channel choice strategy (write or speak)
- Culture strategy (cultural variables)

If you are writing,

- To enhance the writing process → See Chapter II
  - Compose efficiently
  - Overcome writing problems
- To write effectively on macro level → See Chapter III
  - Document design
  - Structural signposts
  - Paragraphs or sections
- To write effectively on the micro level → See Chapter IV
  - Editing for brevity
  - Editing for style
- To use business formats → See Appendix A
  - Memos, reports, letters
- To write correctly → See Appendixes B–D
  - Correct grammar and punctuation

If you are speaking,

- To structure what you say → See Chapter V
  - Tell/sell presentations
  - Questions and answers
  - Consult/join meetings
  - Special situations
- To use effective visual aids → See Chapter VI
  - Visual aid design
  - Visual aid equipment
  - Visual aid usage
- To improve your nonverbal delivery skills → See Chapter VII
  - Tell/sell delivery skills
  - Consult/join facilitation skills

CHAPTER II OUTLINE

I. Composing under normal circumstances
   1. Gather information
   2. Organize your thoughts
   3. Focus the message
   4. Draft the document
   5. Edit the document

II. Composing under special circumstances
   1. Overcoming writer's block
   2. Writing in groups

CHAPTER II

Writing: Composing Efficiently

One of the biggest differences between business writing and other kinds of writing is that business writers usually write under severe time pressures; therefore, increasing your writing efficiency is extremely important. This chapter explains how to make the writing process more efficient by (1) composing efficiently and (2) dealing with the special challenges of writer's block and group writing.

WRITING: COMPOSING EFFICIENTLY		
Section in this chapter:	**I. Composing Under Normal Circumstances**	**II. Composing Under Special Circumstances**
Goal:	To write faster	To overcome special writing challenges

I. COMPOSING UNDER NORMAL CIRCUMSTANCES

WRITING: COMPOSING EFFICIENTLY		
Section in this chapter:	**I. Composing Under Normal Circumstances**	**II. Composing Under Special Circumstances**
Goal:	To write faster	To overcome special writing challenges

Before you sit down and start writing, make some decisions and set some expectations for yourself.

- *Deciding whether to write or not:* Review the variables in the communication strategy explained in the previous chapter, and give some thought to a basic strategic issue: should you write or not? (1) Do you have an important reason to write? (2) Is writing too rigid? Do you want to solidify what may be temporary feelings on the matter? (3) Is writing too risky? Are you sure you want a permanent record? (4) Do you need to see your audience's reactions immediately? (5) Given your audience's situation, is this the right time to be writing? (6) Are you the right person to be writing this document?
- *Differentiating activities:* Once you decide it is appropriate to write, you will be more efficient if you can differentiate the five activities in the writing process: (1) gathering, (2) organizing, (3) focusing, (4) drafting, and (5) editing. Each of these activities calls for different skills.
- *Expecting overlap:* At the same time that you differentiate these stages, do not expect them to occur in lockstep order. Instead, during any one of these stages, be prepared to loop back, to rethink, to make changes. For example, once you've focused your ideas, you may find you need to collect more information for certain topics; or, once you've completed a draft, you may discover you need to reorganize some of your ideas. If you expect this kind of intelligent flexibility, you will take it in stride when the need for it occurs.

A helpful way to visualize the composition process, adopted from writing expert Donald Murray, is shown on the illustration below. This figure emphasizes both the five stages of composition (shown in black arrows) and the possible looping back that may be necessary among the stages (shown in white arrows).

COMPOSING EFFICIENTLY

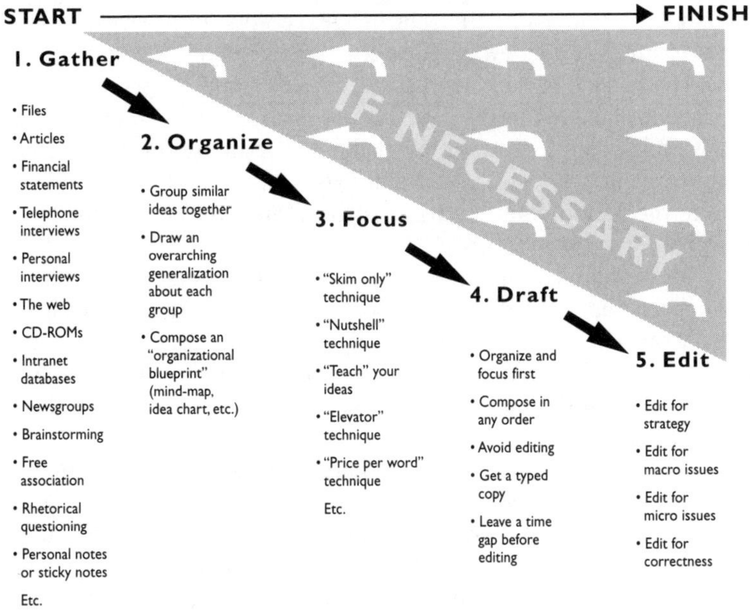

START → FINISH

IF NECESSARY

1. Gather

- Files
- Articles
- Financial statements
- Telephone interviews
- Personal interviews
- The web
- CD-ROMs
- Intranet databases
- Newsgroups
- Brainstorming
- Free association
- Rhetorical questioning
- Personal notes or sticky notes

Etc.

2. Organize

- Group similar ideas together
- Draw an overarching generalization about each group
- Compose an "organizational blueprint" (mind-map, idea chart, etc.)

3. Focus

- "Skim only" technique
- "Nutshell" technique
- "Teach" your ideas
- "Elevator" technique
- "Price per word" technique

Etc.

4. Draft

- Organize and focus first
- Compose in any order
- Avoid editing
- Get a typed copy
- Leave a time gap before editing

5. Edit

- Edit for strategy
- Edit for macro issues
- Edit for micro issues
- Edit for correctness

1. Gather information

As you can see on the illustration above, the first step in the writing process is to gather information. You may want to collect information by synthesizing it from a variety of sources such as reading files, financial statements, or print-outs; interviewing; or accessing information from the web or intranet databases. Another way to gather information is more intuitive: brainstorming (by yourself or with others), free writing (forcing yourself to write for a certain amount of time, even if it doesn't make any sense), or keeping journals or notes on the project (to jot down ideas wherever or whenever they occur to you).

2. Organize your thoughts

Once you have gathered sufficient information, group similar ideas together, draw an overarching generalization about each group, and compose some kind of "organizational blueprint." This blueprint might take a variety of forms: (1) a traditional linear outline, with Roman numerals, capital letters, and so forth; (2) a circular mind map, with the main point in the middle and subordinate points drawn like spokes around the circle using different images, colors, print sizes, arrows, and so forth; (3) a sideways idea chart, with subordinate points displayed to the side of each main point; (4) a pyramid-shaped idea chart, with subordinate points displayed below each main point, or (5) Gantt charts, index cards, sticky notes, computer outlining software, or any other form that works for you. Refer to the Buzon book on *Mind Mapping* or the Minto book on the *Pyramid Principal*, both in the bibliography, for further details.

Most composition experts recommend that your "organizational blueprint" be in the form of a visual idea chart, instead of linear traditional outline, so you can (1) literally see the different levels of ideas and how parts fit together, (2) modify it easily, and (3) be more likely to come up with new ideas. The example on the facing page shows such a visual idea chart.

As you compose your idea chart, keep in mind three rules of thumb: (1) *Each top-level idea summarizes:* Make sure any higher-level idea generalizes about and summarizes all the lower-level ideas branching out below it. (2) *All same-level branches are equivalent:* Check that all branches at the same level are the same kind of idea—for example, all reasons, all steps, all problems, or all recommendations. (3) *Same-level branches are limited in number:* Your audience's short-term working memory and their attention span can handle only five to seven main points. Therefore, group no more than five to nine main branches on any level.

In addition, as you compose your idea chart, keep in mind the message strategy techniques discussed on pages 18–22.

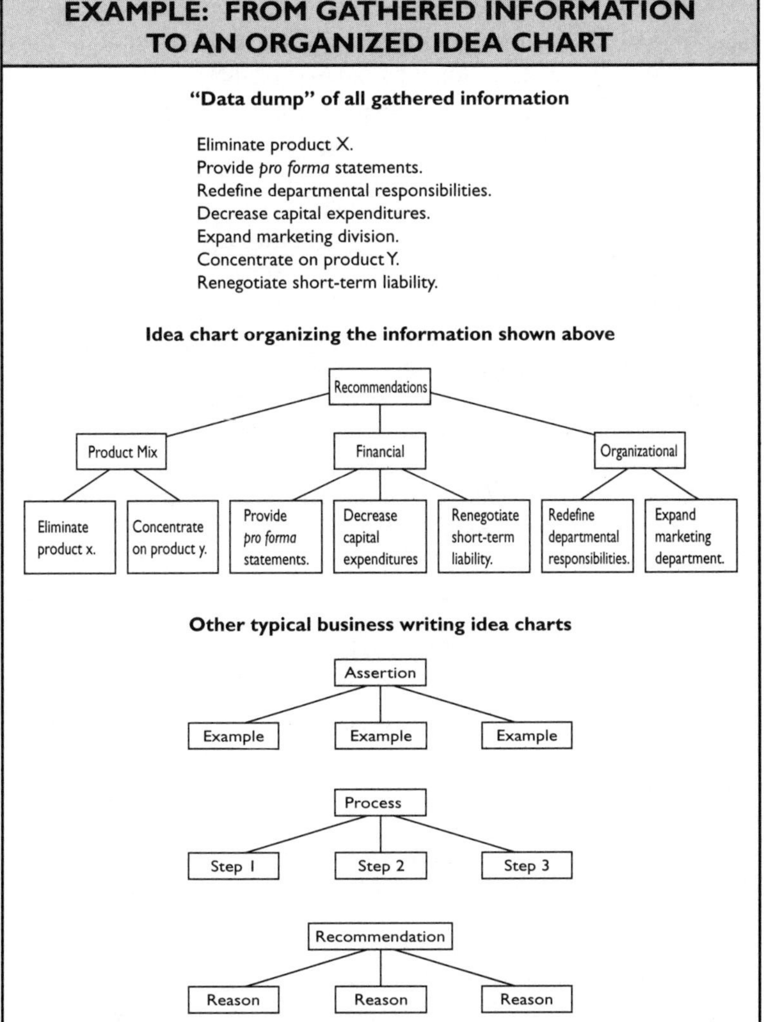
EXAMPLE: FROM GATHERED INFORMATION TO AN ORGANIZED IDEA CHART
"Data dump" of all gathered information
Eliminate product X.
Provide pro forma statements.
Redefine departmental responsibilities.
Decrease capital expenditures.
Expand marketing division.
Concentrate on product Y.
Renegotiate short-term liability.
Idea chart organizing the information shown above
Recommendations
Product Mix
Financial
Organizational
Eliminate product x.
Concentrate on product y.
Provide pro forma statements.
Decrease capital expenditures
Renegotiate short-term liability.
Redefine departmental responsibilities.
Expand marketing department.
Other typical business writing idea charts
Assertion
Example
Example
Example
Process
Step 1
Step 2
Step 3
Recommendation
Reason
Reason
Reason

3. Focus the message

Now, step back from the details and try to see the essence of the message. Here are some techniques to focus your ideas.

- *Imagine the reader skimming*: Ask yourself, "What does my audience need to know most? If they only skim my message, what is the absolute minimum they should learn?"
- *"Nutshell" your ideas*: In the words of writing expert Linda Flower, "nutshell" your ideas. In a few sentences—that is, in a nutshell—lay out your main ideas. Distinguish major and minor ideas and decide how they are all related.
- *"Teach" your ideas*: Once you can express your ideas in a nutshell to yourself, think about how you would teach those ideas to someone else. Like nutshelling, figuring out how you would teach your ideas helps you form concepts in such a way that your audience gets the point, not just a list of facts.
- *Use the "elevator" technique*: Another way to focus your ideas is to imagine meeting your audience in the top-floor elevator. You have only the time it takes the elevator to descend to explain your main ideas. What would you say?
- *Use the "busy boss" technique*: Imagine your boss or client catches you in the hall and says "I have to leave for the airport and I don't have time to read your document. Tell me the main ideas in two minutes."

At this stage in the process, you will have an organized, focused list. For example, you might have a list of three to five steps in a procedure, examples supporting a conclusion, component parts of a process, chronological list of events, reasons why they should buy this product, or recommendations for approval. Upon analyzing this focused list, you may find you need to go back and gather additional information.

Although the writing process is recursive, be sure to complete the first three stages, generally referred to as "prewriting" (gathering, organizing, and focusing), before you start composing. Experts observe that effective writers spend about 50% of their time on prewriting activities, as opposed to drafting and editing.

4. Draft the document

The key to effective drafting is to let your creativity flow. Don't try to draft and edit at the same time. Don't be a perfectionist; don't try to write a perfect product the first time. Here are some techniques to help you in the drafting stage.

Compose in any order. Don't force yourself to write from the beginning of your document straight through to the end. Instead, write the sections you are most comfortable with first. You don't need to write your introduction first. Writing the introduction may be a formidable task, and you often end up having to change it anyway, if you modify your ideas or organizations as you compose the rest of the draft. Therefore, many writing experts advise writing your introduction last.

Avoid editing. Drafting should be creative, not overly analytical. Do not worry about specific problems as you write your draft. Do not edit. If you cannot think of a word, leave a blank space; if you cannot decide between two words, write them both down. Circle or put a check mark in the margin next to awkward or unclear sections, and come back to them later.

Print a typed copy. Get your draft onto typed copy—one side only, double spaced, with wide margins. You will draft faster if you avoid writing by hand: you write in longhand at about 15 words per minute; you can type at 20 to 60 words per minute; you can dictate into a machine or voice recognition software at 65 to 95 words per minute. Furthermore, you will edit faster working from typed copy. Printing a hard copy will also allow you to overcome the prevalent problem of editing only the section you can see at one time on your monitor instead of editing the entire document.

Schedule a time gap. You will do a better job of editing if you leave some time between the creative drafting and analytical editing stages, so your thoughts can incubate subconsciously. For important or complex documents, separate the two stages by an overnight break. Even if you are under severe time constraints, or if you are composing a routine document, leave yourself a short gap: for example, begin editing after a lunch break or even a five- to ten-minute break.

5. Edit the document

When you begin editing, don't immediately begin to agonize over commas and word choices. Instead, complete the four-step plan that follows—using a hard copy of the entire document at once, not just what you can see at one time on your computer screen. This four-step plan will save you time because you won't waste time perfecting sections you may decide to cut or change substantially.

1. Edit for strategy. Before you begin fine-tuning, review the document for the communication strategy issues discussed in Chapter I: (1) the communicator strategy, (2) the audience strategy, (3) the message strategy, and (4) the culture strategy.

2. Edit for macro issues. Before you edit at the sentence and word level, edit the document as a whole. Specifically, review the issues covered in Chapter III: (1) document design for "high skim value," (2) structural signposts for linkage, and (3) effective paragraphs or sections.

3. Edit for micro issues. Once you have edited at the strategic and macro levels, then edit your sentences and words, as discussed in Chapter IV: (1) avoiding wordiness and overlong sentences, and (2) using an appropriate style. In addition, check your format for consistency, as explained in Appendix A.

4. Edit for correctness. If you have any specific questions on grammar or punctuation, refer to the appendices at the end of this book.

Proofread carefully. Don't confuse computer proofreading for human proofreading. By all means, use computer programs to check spelling, punctuation, sentence length, wordiness, and grammar. However, computers cannot check for logic, flow, emphasis, tone, or computer-generated errors such as transferring only a part of a section or not deleting a phrase you changed. Computers cannot even check all spelling errors (e.g., *you* when you meant to write *your* or *on* when you meant to write *of*). Finally, computers cannot catch missing words or phrases.

Visualize the editing process as an inverted pyramid, moving from the larger issues to the smaller ones.

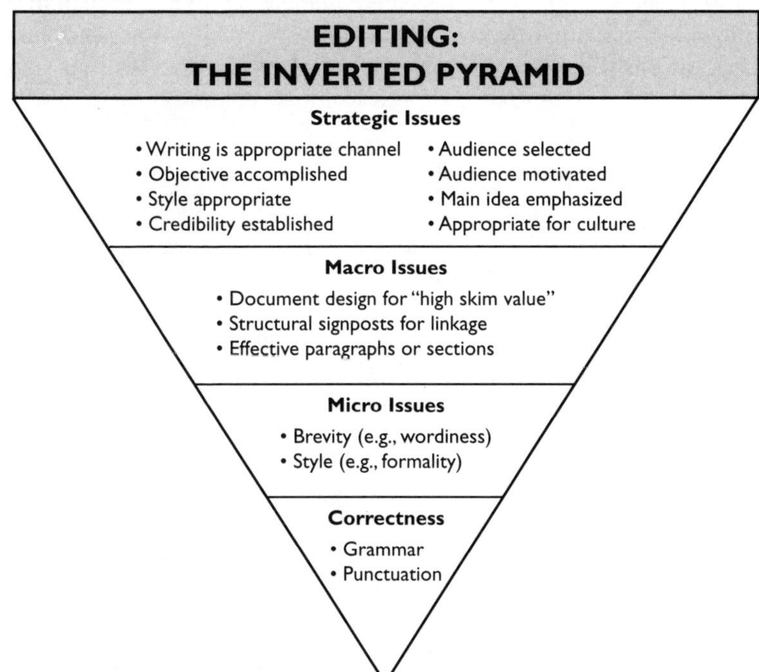

EDITING:
THE INVERTED PYRAMID
Strategic Issues
• Writing is appropriate channel
• Objective accomplished
• Style appropriate
• Credibility established
• Audience selected
• Audience motivated
• Main idea emphasized
• Appropriate for culture
Macro Issues
• Document design for "high skim value"
• Structural signposts for linkage
• Effective paragraphs or sections
Micro Issues
• Brevity (e.g., wordiness)
• Style (e.g., formality)
Correctness
• Grammar
• Punctuation

II. COMPOSING UNDER SPECIAL CIRCUMSTANCES

WRITING: COMPOSING EFFICIENTLY		
Section in this chapter:	**I. Composing Under Normal Circumstances**	**II. Composing Under Special Circumstances**
Goal:	To write faster	To overcome special writing challenges

This section offers some ideas on how to deal with two special challenges in writing: (1) overcoming writer's block and (2) writing in collaboration with a group.

1. Overcoming writer's block

Writer's block is a temporary inability to write: you sit there facing the blank screen or the blank page and can't get any words out. Virtually everyone has experienced writer's block at one time or another. Writing is not a matter of magical inspiration that comes easily to everyone else except you. If you're stuck, try one or more of these techniques.

Change the writing task. One set of techniques centers on changing the writing task you are working on at that particular moment.

- *Write another section first.* If you are stuck on one section, put it aside and write another section first. Don't force yourself to write from beginning to end. Write any section that seems easier first—even if it's the conclusion.
- *Write your headings first.* Try writing your headings, subheadings, or bullet points first. Then, go back and flesh out each one.
- *Resketch your idea chart.* Some people think better visually than they do verbally. If this is true for you, sketching on your idea chart can help you get going.
- *Work on nontext issues.* Work on some other part of the writing task, such as formatting or graphics, so you can have some sense of accomplishment before returning to text writing.

Change your activity. Another set of techniques has to do with changing the kind of activity you are engaged in.

- *Take a break.* If you are bogged down with your ideas or expression, taking a break often helps. Walk away. Do something else. Allow time for the problems to incubate in your mind subconsciously. When you return after this rest period, you will often be able to work more effectively.
- *"Talk" to your reader.* Sit back and imagine that you are talking to your readers. Then, write what you would say to them. Often, wording will flow more easily and less awkwardly when you talk out loud than when you write silently.
- *Talk about your ideas.* To use this technique, talk with someone else about your writing. Discuss your ideas, or your overall organization, or specific points—whatever seems to be eluding you.
- *Read or talk about something else.* Read something else. Talk to someone about something else. Some people find that changing activities in this way allows their thoughts to develop.

Change your perceptions. A final set of techniques involves changing your perceptions about yourself and about writing.

- *Relax your commitment to rules.* Sometimes writers are blocked by what they perceive as hard-and-fast "rules," such as "Never use the word *I* in business writing." Reject these rules, especially during the drafting stage. You can always edit later on.
- *Break down the project.* Reorganize the entire writing project into a series of more manageable parts.
- *Print draft at the top of each page.* Print the word *draft* at the top of each page, or lightly in the background of each page to remind yourself that you don't have to be perfect.
- *Relax your expectations.* Avoid being too self-critical. Lower unrealistic expectations for yourself. Try a relaxation technique from those described on pages 150–155.
- *Don't fall in love with your prose.* Just get something down. It doesn't have to be perfect; you may have to edit it anyway.
- *Expect complexity.* Writing is so complex that you should not expect it to go logically and smoothly, but rather to involve continual rethinking and changing. Keep in mind the illustration on page 37.

2. Writing in groups

Group writing is increasingly prevalent in business. Collaborating means compromising; but it also means benefiting from a wealth of talents and differing degrees of credibility. Here are some suggestions for writing effectively and efficiently in groups.

Agree on group guidelines. Before you start in on the writing project itself, agree on guidelines and ground rules for the group to function effectively. (See pages 95–103.) Decide who will facilitate the meetings, how you will make decisions for various items, how you will deal with emotional "ownership" of wording, and how you will deal with infractions of group agreements and refusals to change. Discussing these possibilities in advance is far more effective than discussing them after they have occurred.

Agree on the tasks and time line. Once you have agreed on general guidelines for the group, set the specific time line and writing tasks. Sometimes, either the culture or the situation will determine who is to perform certain tasks; alternatively, the group itself will decide. As you delineate the tasks and time line, decide if and how you might use groupware (e.g., to edit various drafts of the document). Specify deadlines, yet try to build some leeway. Finally, remember to specify what milestones you will use to identify progress and modify the time line, if necessary. The six tasks to include on your time line follow.

Setting the strategy Agree on a time frame for, and specify who will be involved in, setting the communication strategy—communicator strategy, audience strategy, message strategy, and culture strategy—as summarized on the checklist on page 32.

Gathering information Most groups divide the research tasks based on the interests and expertise of each member. Remember to set times for periodic meetings during the research phase to pool ideas, avoid unnecessary overlap, and move together toward conclusions and recommendations.

Organizing and focusing the information Set a time to organize and focus the information, as described on pages 38–40. With group writing, it is especially important to do so extremely clearly before you start writing. As a group, collaborate on the structure, outline, or idea chart before anyone starts drafting.

Drafting the document Next on the time line comes the drafting stage. Consider two options here.

- *Use various draft writers.* One choice is to have different people write different sections. This option is most appropriate if you want to spread the responsibility, if the writers' styles are similar, or if people want to write the section of their expertise. If you use multiple draft writers, be sure to (1) agree about formality, directness, and other style issues in advance, (2) allow enough time to edit for consistency after all the drafts are complete, and (3) to avoid a "smorgasbord" in which every item that every team member has learned is tossed into the final document.
- *Use one writer.* A second option is to use one writer, who writes the entire document from scratch. This option assures you of a more consistent style throughout, avoids ownership issues with various sections, and takes advantage of a gifted writer; however, it centralizes power and responsibility with one person. If you are using one writer, be sure to (1) include him or her in the research progress meetings throughout the process, and (2) allow enough time to incorporate group revisions after the draft.

Editing the document Be sure to allow enough time for editing the document. Some groups waste time arguing about every detail of editing; others don't leave enough time to edit at all. Instead, consider these two options.

- *Use a single editor.* One choice is to use one editor—either a group member, a colleague, or a professional. If you do so, schedule enough time for him or her to edit. Agree clearly whether you want (1) a copy editor for typos, spelling, and grammar only, or (2) a style editor for consistency in style and format only, or (3) an analytic editor for strategy and content changes.
- *Use a group of editors.* A second choice is to edit as a group. Circulate hard copy or electronic copy for each group member to read and annotate. Then, (1) the group can meet face to face or electronically to discuss all editing issues, (2) one person can read all the comments and decide what to incorporate, or (3) the group can discuss strategy and content issues only, delegating style editing and copy editing to one person.

Attending to final details Finally, don't forget to build into the time line any time needed for proofreading, gaining approval of the final document if necessary, and producing and distributing the document.

CHAPTER III OUTLINE

I. Document design for "high skim value"
   1. Using headings and subheadings
   2. Using white space
   3. Choosing typography

II. Structural signposts for linkage
   1. In the opening and closing
   2. Throughout the document

III. Effective paragraphs or sections

CHAPTER III

Writing: Macro Issues

The previous chapter covered methods to save time and organize clearly—for yourself. This chapter will cover methods to save time and demonstrate that organization clearly—for your reader. Thus, the writing techniques in this chapter are based on using the organizational techniques in the preceding chapter.

The issues covered in this chapter are called *macrowriting*—because they pertain to writing on the macro level; that is, for the document as a whole. The first macrowriting method is using document design techniques for "high skim value," so busy business readers can skim your document. (In some rare cases, because of the culture or the context, these "high skim value" techniques would not be appropriate.) The second macrowriting method is using "structural signposts" so readers can see the linkage between your ideas. The third is using effective paragraphs or sections so readers can understand the text easily.

MACROWRITING			
Section in this chapter:	**I. Document Design for "High Skim Value"**	**II. Structural Signposts for Linkage**	**III. Effective Paragraphs or Sections**
Goal:	To increase readability, show organization	To show logical flow	To organize paragraphs or sections
Methods:	Headings White space Typography	Throughout the document Openings/closings	Generalization and support Structural signposts

This chapter covers *macrowriting*, pertaining to the document as a whole; the following chapter will cover *microwriting*, pertaining to sentence and word choice. Please note that all of these macro and micro issues apply equally to all kinds of business documents—including memos, reports, and letters. See Appendix A, pages 163–169, for descriptions of these standard business formats.

I. DOCUMENT DESIGN FOR "HIGH SKIM VALUE"

MACROWRITING			
Section in this chapter:	**I. Document Design for "High Skim Value"**	**II. Structural Signposts for Linkage**	**III. Effective Paragraphs or Sections**
Goal:	To increase readability, show organization	To show logical flow	To organize paragraphs or sections
Methods:	Headings White space Typography	Throughout the document Openings/closings	Generalization and support Structural signposts

Because many business readers will only skim your document, or only read certain sections of it carefully, using document design techniques ensures that they will notice your important points if they do skim, and that they will be able to find sections of particular interest for more careful reading or reference. In addition, document design techniques make your document more appealing and inviting to read. Three techniques for document design include using (1) headings and subheadings, (2) white space, and (3) typography.

1. Using headings and subheadings

Just as the top-level ideas on your idea chart (explained on pages 38–39) showed your main ideas for yourself as you composed, those same top-level ideas become revised into headings and subheadings to show the main ideas to your reader. To write effective headings and subheadings, use "stand-alone sense," parallel form, and limited wording.

Stand-alone sense "Stand-alone sense" means the headings and subheadings make sense on their own, capturing the essence of your ideas. A reader should be able to read your headings and subheadings only and understand them without reading the rest of the document.

Ineffective heading: does not make "stand-alone sense"

Recommendation

Effective heading: makes "stand-alone sense"

Recommendation: Build the new plant in Pittsburgh

Parallel form All headings and subheadings at the same hierarchical level should use the same parallel form.

Grammatical parallelism One kind of parallelism is grammatical—that is, the same grammatical construction for ideas of equal importance. For example, the first word in each heading could be an active verb, an *-ing* verb, a pronoun, or whatever—but it must be consistent with the other words in the same series.

Ineffective heading: three steps are not parallel

Steps to organize internally

1. Establishing formal sales organization.
2. Production department: responsibilities defined.
3. Improve cost-accounting system.

Effective heading: three steps are parallel

Steps to organize internally

1. Establish formal sales organization.
2. Define responsibilities within the production department.
3. Improve cost-accounting system.

Conceptual parallelism Headings must be not only grammatically parallel, but also conceptually parallel—that is, each heading should be the same kind of item.

Ineffective headings: not conceptually parallel, although grammatically parallel

Cost-Effective Optimization

- What are the options?
- What are the problems with Testing?
- What is Finite Element Analysis (FEA)?
- What are the benefits of FEA?

Effective headings: conceptually parallel

Cost-Effective Optimization

- Option 1: Testing
- Option 2: FEA

2. Using white space

The term *white space* refers to empty space on the page. White space shows your organization and section breaks visually, emphasizes important ideas, and presents your ideas in more manageable bits. Readers unconsciously react favorably toward white space, so think about how you might allow for it in the following ways:

Shorter blocks of text Business readers generally do not want to see large, formidable blocks of text. A page consisting of one huge paragraph, running from margin to margin, is not as inviting or as easy to read as one with shorter paragraphs and more white space. Therefore, keep most of your paragraphs short, averaging not more than about 150–200 words, five sentences, or $1\frac{1}{2}$ inches of single-spaced typing. On the other hand, the page will look monotonous if all the paragraphs are the same length, so vary the length of your paragraphs.

Ineffective use of white space: paragraph too long

> If you consistently write very long paragraphs, your reader may just look at the page and say "Forget it! Why should I wade through all the material to pick out the important points?" And why should your reader do that work? Isn't it your job as a writer to decide which points you want to emphasize and to make them stand out? You may want to show the creative gushing process you go through as a writer and just go on and on writing as ideas come into your head. Your psychologist, your friends, or your family might possibly be very interested in how this process works. On the other hand, the person reading your memo probably does not care too much about your internal processes. The business reader wants to see your main ideas quickly and to have the work of sorting out done for him or her. Didn't you find that just the look of this paragraph rather put you off? Did it make you want to read on? Or did it make you want to give up?

Effective use of white space and paragraph length

> Medium-sized paragraphs or sections are easier for your reader to comprehend if you
>
> - have a general topic sentence or heading at the beginning,
> - include support sentences that amplify that generalization,
> - use bullet points like these if you want to show a list.

Indentations Sometimes you can use white space to show the relationship among your sections—by indenting increasingly subordinate information to the right or by setting off your opening and closing.

Example: indentations to show headings versus subheadings

FIRST MAIN HEADING
This section is not indented. It is typed flush with the left margin. Smsnsbb sjvlreovrkio vjaikrh vaohdb akdjhbidhvbkfbv

First Subheading
Here is the first subsection. Note that the entire subsection is indented. woshp nrkhqei jkbpire akjr sjh fjgui tkjtrg hithtw tjwhr ejq

Second Subheading
jdn qplsms neonbfo enr eoj dsnla eow jf ejfefef fnnenfef nfe nfw qfw fwfefe mpq

SECOND MAIN HEADING
Now that we are back to a main heading, we type flush with the left margin again. kdm nfhv eh cidh lsp

"Ragged right" margins Usually, choose "ragged right" margins (that is, margins that are uneven on the right side of the page) instead of "justified" margins (that is, margins that end evenly on the right side) for two reasons. First, justified margins make it harder for your readers' eye to distinguish one line from another. Second, justified margins often produce variable random white spaces (called "rivers" of space) between words that irritate and slow down your reader. So, use justified margins only if you have desktop publishing equipment that does not leave these random spaces.

Lists Using lists is another way to increase the white space on the page and make your document easier to follow. Effective lists must be both grammatically and conceptually parallel as explained on page 51. Remember to limit lists to no more than seven points.

Using lists for emphasis Use lists only for those items you want to emphasize visually.

Ineffective example: no list, less white space

> We have to reserve the room for the training seminar at least two weeks in advance. I'm worried about getting the facilitator confirmed by then. We also need to print up posters announcing the session. Will you take care of these arrangements? Don't forget that the poster should include the room number, too.

Effective example: uses list and white space for emphasis

> I just wanted to remind you about the three arrangements you agreed to handle for the training seminar:
>
> 1. Line up the facilitator and set the seminar date.
> 2. Reserve the room by November 15.
> 3. Print up the posters (including the room number) by December 1.

Choosing numbers versus bullets Lists can begin with numbers or with bullet points (that is, large dots, asterisks, or hyphens to set off items). Use bullet points if the list is not in order of importance or in time sequence. On the other hand, use numbers if the list implies a time sequence, if the list is in order of importance, or if you will need to refer to items by number.

Indenting lists Lists are easier to read if the entire numbered or bullet-pointed section is indented.

Effective example: list indentation

> • Here is an example of a bullet-pointed sentence in which every line is indented so the bullet point stands out on its own.

Ineffective examples: list indentation

> • Here is an example of an ineffective bullet-pointed sentence because the subsequent lines "wrap around" the bullet.
>
> • Here is another example of an ineffective bullet-pointed sentence because only the first line is indented.

3. Choosing typography

Typography—the use of boldface, italics, underlining, fonts, sizes, and capitals—is another important document design tool to enhance high skim value. Avoid the potential danger of overusing typography, which will make important ideas no longer stand out. Instead, when choosing typography, think about issues of consistency and readability.

Using typography consistently Use typography for important ideas and consistent patterns.

- *For important ideas only:* Use typography only for those words and phrases you want you reader to be able to skim. Generally, this means reserving typography for headings only, not using it for random words that a reader's voice might inflect spread throughout the document. If you find yourself wanting to italicize a word or phrase midparagraph, that's usually a sign that you need to bring that word or phrase up front as a heading. Don't overuse any typography used for emphasis; it will tire the reader's eyes.
- *In a consistent pattern:* Set a pattern and stick to it. For example, if you start off using boldface for your main headings and underlining for your secondary headings, continue to do so exactly throughout the document, so you don't confuse your reader's expectations. Make sure your headings at each level look different from the headings at other levels, so you establish a visual pattern.

Choosing a serif font In general, serif fonts are the easiest to read for extended text. Serif fonts are those, like the one you are reading right now, with extenders on the end of most letters. They are usually easier to read, because these extenders give the eye more to "wrap around" and can, therefore, be processed more quickly. They are extremely pervasive for text in business documents.

Choose a serif font, like this one.

Sans serif fonts do not have extenders on the ends of letters. They usually take the reader longer to read, because this lack of extenders gives the eye less to wrap around. These fonts are used mostly for short phrases, especially in advertisements, because of their less formal, less traditional, appearance.

Avoid a sans serif font, like this one, for extended text.

Choosing readable typography Readable typography, as described below, is faster for your reader to process.

Limit the use of all capitals Because use of all capitals retards reading speed, limit the use of all capital letters to strings of three or four words. Upper- and lowercase is easier to read than all capitals; all capitals lose their heading effectiveness in large blocks of text.

> AVOID OVERUSED CAPS. THIS PARAGRAPH TENDS TO RUN TOGETHER BECAUSE EVERY WORD IS TYPED IN ALL CAPITAL LETTERS. NO ONE PHRASE STANDS OUT.
>
> USE CAPS APPROPRIATELY. This paragraph more clearly tells the reader to avoid all caps by using them selectively, only in the heading.

Especially avoid all capital letters in a sans serif type.

> DO NOT USE A SAN SERIF FONT, WITH ALL CAPITAL LETTERS, AS IN THIS EXAMPLE. THE LACK OF SIZE VARIATION WITH ALL CAPITALS AND NO SERIFS MAKES THE TEXT QUITE DIFFICULT TO READ.
>
> This is serif font, with a capital letter only at the beginning of each sentence. The text is easier to read because there is more size variation; it does not all run together.

Use boldface or larger typeface over italics When choosing a typeface to use for headings or subheadings, choose boldface or larger typeface rather than italics because they are faster to process than italics.

> *Italics are harder to read because they are slanted and lighter than regular type. Italics are fine for headings, but not for extended text.*

Use proportional type

> This is proportional type. Each word appears more readily because there is more white space between each word than between each letter.
>
> `Nonproportional type, like this, puts too much white space within each word. The reader's eye has to spend additional time seeking out each word.`

Choosing a readable size Avoid downsizing the type to the proverbial "fine print" to make something fit on the page. Generally, avoid point sizes of 9 or lower except in very short bursts; use 10-point type with caution; use 12-point type for most business documents.

> Do not use 9-point type like this for extended text.

II. STRUCTURAL SIGNPOSTS FOR LINKAGE

MACROWRITING			
Section in this chapter:	**I. Document Design for "High Skim Value"**	**II. Structural Signposts for Linkage**	**III. Effective Paragraphs or Sections**
Goal:	To increase readability, show organization	To show logical flow	To organize paragraphs or sections
Methods:	Headings White space Typography	Throughout the document Openings/closings	Generalization and support Structural signposts

In addition to using document design techniques to make it easier for your reader to see your main points, use structural signposts to make it easier for your reader to see your logical flow. Provide such signposts (1) throughout the document and (2) in your opening and closing.

1. Throughout the document

Make it easier for your reader to read quickly by providing linkages between the main sections with (1) back-and-forth references, (2) section previews, and (3) document design.

Back-and-forth references Pause periodically to let the reader know where you've been and where you next plan to go—at least at the end or the beginning of each major section. Pick up a key word or phrase from the previous section, and use it in the opening of the next section. Here are some examples:

Examples: Using back-and-forth references

> If you adopt this new marketing plan (reference backward to previous section), you can expect the following financial results (reference forward to upcoming section).
>
> Implementing this organizational structure (reference backward) requires addressing each of the major stakeholder groups (reference forward).
>
> Given these inefficiencies in the current procedure (reference backward), we recommend adopting the following new process (reference forward).

Section previews If you are writing a longer document, use section previews as another way to link your ideas clearly for your reader. *Section previews* are sentences or phrases that provide a preview of the forthcoming section. The following example shows how a section preview looks at the beginning of each new section.

Example: Using section previews

> This is the introduction. It builds reader receptivity, tells your purpose for writing, and gives a preview, like this: (1) Section 1, (2) Section 2, and (3) Section 3.
>
> **Section Heading 1**
>
> The introduction to each section should also let your reader know the preview for the section, such as this section covers first subsection and second subsection.
>
> *First subsection heading*
>
> If you had third-level headings, you would introduce them in a preview sentence or phrase here—and so on throughout your document.

Document design techniques Finally, your document design itself can show your reader how your ideas relate by their placement on the page. For a one-page document, use of indentation forms an *I* shape, going in and out on the left margin, to differentiate the opening and closing sections visually, as shown below.

Example: using document design

> This paragraph is the opening for a short document. Dk fjh tyfhg dbmo ldpwld oepls mskeg iokun gefre.
>
> - First heading: vne ekee essts akka llla skes shewa kkklawia wosloasp aslekase bde kisas skssdrew ss
> - Second heading: sesei poze yoease seib aawe akka vne ekee assel as aslekase bde kisas skes shewa kkklawia
> - Third heading: kisas skes kisas skssdrew vne ekee essts akka llla skes shewa kkklawia wosloasp aslekase bde kisas
>
> The reader can easily see that this paragraph, once again flush to the left margin, is the closing.

2. In the opening and closing

Because the opening and closing are the most prominent places in your document, they are important places to show how your ideas link together.

Opening Your introduction is a key place to set up the underlying logical flow for the rest of the document. An effective introduction accomplishes three aims.

- *Builds reader interest ("what exists"):* One method to build reader interest and receptivity is to refer to an existing situation, to establish a context. For example,

  > As we discussed last Tuesday,
  >
  > As you know, we are currently planning for the new fiscal year.

  You may also wish to refer to ideas shared with the reader, to establish a common ground (as discussed on page 16). For example,

  > We don't want to sacrifice long-term profits for short-term gains.
  >
  > We need to improve market share.

- *Explains your purpose for writing ("why write"):* Let your readers know your reason or purpose for writing—so they can read with that purpose in mind. For example,

  > This report summarizes the results of our fourth-quarter sales.
  >
  > I am writing to solicit your opinion on this proposal.

- *Provides a preview ("how organized"):* Include a brief "table of contents," so your readers will be able to comprehend your writing more easily and to choose specific sections for reference, if they wish. If the document is short and organized around one group of ideas on your idea tree (see pages 38–39), then include a preview such as this one:

  > This memo covers five steps in the new procedure.

  If, on the other hand, your document is long and organized around many different groups of ideas on your idea tree, then include a more explicit preview that lists your section headings, such as this one:

  > This report is divided into three main sections: (1) what equipment you need, (2) how to use the equipment, and (3) how to maintain the equipment.

  If you use this explicit kind of list in your introduction, then use exactly the same wording in your main headings as you did for the items on your "how organized" list.

Although an effective introduction includes each of these elements, you may present them in any order, depending on your credibility and your audience's needs as discussed on pages 8–17.

- *Purpose or preview first:* If you have high credibility or if your audience is indifferent or likely to agree with your message, state your preview or purpose first.
- *Build reader interest first:* If you have lower credibility or are less sure of your audience's agreement, build reader interest and receptivity first.

How long should an introduction be? Long documents might include a paragraph or two for each of the three aims. Short documents, on the other hand, might open with one sentence that accomplishes all three aims:

> As you requested last Tuesday (= "what exists"), I have summarized (= "why write") my three objections to the new marketing plan (= "how organized").

Closing When you reach the end of your document, your reader needs a sense of closure, and you need to reinforce your communication objective and leave your reader with a strong final impression. Two ways to do so include the following:

- *Feedback mechanism* such as "I will call you next Tuesday to discuss this matter."
- *"What next" step* such as "If you wish to apply, please return the enclosed application by January 15."

Two pitfalls to avoid in the closing include (1) introducing a completely new topic that might divert your reader's attention from your communication objective or (2) apologizing or undercutting your argument at the end.

III. EFFECTIVE PARAGRAPHS OR SECTIONS

MACROWRITING			
Section in this chapter:	**I. Document Design for "High Skim Value"**	**II. Structural Signposts for Linkage**	**III. Effective Paragraphs or Sections**
Goal:	To increase readability, show organization	To show logical flow	To organize paragraphs or sections
Methods:	Headings White space Typography	Throughout the document Openings/closings	Generalization and support Structural signposts

A third macro issue in writing has to do with each paragraph or section; each should have (1) generalization and support, with a topic sentence or heading that states the generalization and subsequent sentences to support it, and (2) structural signposts to tie the ideas within each paragraph or section together clearly.

1. Generalization and support

Each paragraph or section should begin with a generalization; every single sentence in the paragraph or section must support that generalization. Readers may not consciously look for a generalization followed by support, but intuitively they expect to see it. If you use this technique, your readers will be able to assimilate information quickly and easily.

Effective: first sentence is a generalization for all support sentences

> This procedure consists of four steps. First, do this. Second, do that. Third, do the other. Finally, do this.

Ineffective: first sentence is not a generalization

> First, do this. Second, do that. Third, do the other. Finally, do this.

Topic sentence or heading State your generalization in either of two ways: for standard prose paragraphs, as a topic sentence; for sections, as a heading or subheading. Here are some examples, showing the same concept as a topic sentence, then as a heading:

Example topic sentences

The new brochures are full of major printing errors.
Three causes contributed to the problem at Plant X.

Example headings

Printing Errors in Brochure
Causes of Plant X Problems

Development The generalization in your topic sentence or heading must be fully supported with sufficient evidence.

Ineffective example: undeveloped paragraphs

Although one-sentence paragraphs are fine when used occasionally for emphasis, if you consistently write in one-sentence paragraphs, you will find they do not develop your ideas.

One-sentence paragraphs also mean you don't group your ideas together logically.

Of course, the preceding sentence belongs in a paragraph with a topic sentence about the drawbacks of one-sentence paragraphs.

Effective example: well-developed paragraph

Consistently writing one-sentence paragraphs presents several drawbacks for your reader. First, your paragraphs will lack development. Second, your ideas will not group together logically. Finally, your writing will be choppy and incoherent.

2. Structural signposts for linkages

Just as you provide linkage among sections in the document as a whole, you also need to provide linkage among the ideas in each paragraph or section. Choose either of the following two techniques: (1) document design techniques and (2) transitional words.

Document design techniques One way to show how your ideas link is to use document design techniques—such as headings and subheadings, bullet points, indentation, and typography—as discussed on pages 55–56. Here is an example:

Example: using document design to show linkage

Recommendations for Financial Crisis

- Cut back drastically on
  - Labor,
  - Outside services,
  - Manufacturing overhead services.
- Do not approach shareholders for more capital.
- Renegotiate short-term liabilities with the banks.

Transitional words A second method is to use transitional words. The example below shows the same information as shown above, but this time written in standard paragraph form using the transitions *first*, *second*, and *third*.

Example: transitional words to show linkage

XYZ Company should follow these recommendations to clear up its financial crisis. First, cut back drastically on labor, outside services, and manufacturing overhead expenses. Second, do not approach shareholders for more capital. Third, renegotiate short-term liabilities with the banks.

Here are some examples of the transitions used most frequently:

FREQUENTLY USED TRANSITIONAL WORDS

To signal	Examples
Addition or amplification	And, furthermore, besides, next, moreover, in addition, again, also, similarly, too, finally, second, subsequently, last
Contrast	But, or, nor, yet, still, however, nevertheless, on the contrary, on the other hand, conversely, although
Example	For example, for instance, such as, thus, that is
Sequence	First, second, third, next, then
Conclusion	Therefore, thus, then, in conclusion, consequently, as a result, accordingly, finally
Time or place	At the same time, simultaneously, above, below, further on, so far, until now

Visualize each paragraph or section as an inverted pyramid, with the heading or topic sentence so broad that it covers all of your supporting ideas.

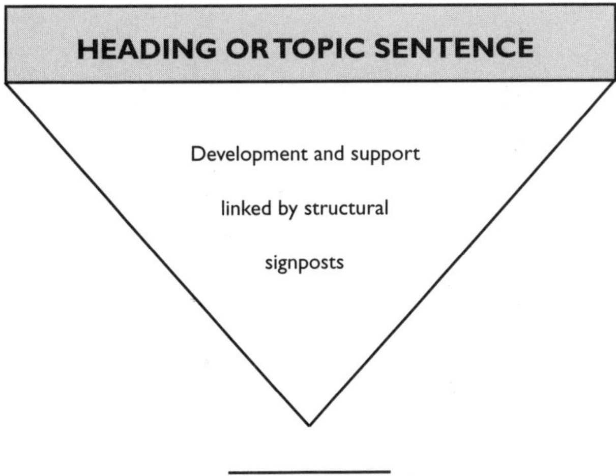

See the checklist on page 82 for a summary of the macrowriting issues covered in this chapter. See the following chapter for a discussion of microwriting issues.

CHAPTER IV OUTLINE

I. Editing for brevity
   1. Avoiding wordiness
   2. Avoiding overlong sentences

II. Choosing a style
   1. Businesslike or bureaucratic?
   2. Active or passive?
   3. Jargon or no jargon?

CHAPTER IV

Writing: Micro Issues

Micro issues in writing have to do with choices about sentences and words. The chart that follows outlines two kinds of micro issues covered in the two sections of this chapter. The first section, on editing for brevity, discusses micro techniques to make your writing more concise. The second section, on choosing a style, has to do with decisions to make your writing style appropriate in a given situation.

MICROWRITING		
Section in this chapter:	**I. Editing for Brevity**	**II. Choosing a Style**
Goal:	To make writing concise	To make tone appropriate
Methods:	Avoiding wordiness Avoiding overlong sentences	Businesslike or bureaucratic? Active or passive? Jargon or no jargon?

If you have microwriting questions concerning correct grammar and punctuation, see Appendixes B through D at the end of this book. See the Writing Checklists at the end of this chapter, pages 82–83, for a summary of all macro and micro writing skills.

I. EDITING FOR BREVITY

MICROWRITING		
Section in this chapter:	**I. Editing for Brevity**	**II. Choosing a Style**
Goal:	To make writing concise	To make tone appropriate
Methods:	Avoiding wordiness Avoiding overlong sentences	Businesslike or bureaucratic? Active or passive? Jargon or no jargon?

One of the advantages of writing is that you can save your audience time—since reading is faster than listening. And, of course, business readers value saving time. Therefore, use the following techniques to make your writing more concise: (1) avoiding wordiness and (2) avoiding overlong sentences.

1. Avoiding wordiness

Avoiding wordiness never means deleting essential information to keep your document short at all costs. Choices about how much or how little information your audience needs are strategic, as explained on page 12.

Instead, avoiding wordiness means omitting unnecessary words and deadwood expressions. By trimming "you are undoubtedly aware of the fact" to "you know," you have saved your reader the trouble of processing five extra words and have communicated the same idea. If you want to avoid wordiness, watch for overused prepositions and overused use of *be* verbs.

"To be or not to be?" Beware of linking verbs. Linking verbs do no more for the sentence than add the equivalent of an equals sign. Overusing them produces wordy, lifeless sentences. The main *linking verbs* are forms of the verb *to be* (including *is*, *was*, *were*, and *will be*); other linking verbs include *become*, *look*, *seem*, *appear*, *sound*, and *feel*.

Problem #1: Overused linking verbs Try circling, or have a computer program highlight, the linking verbs in a sample of your writing, and beware if you find yourself using them in most of your sentences. You need to use these linking verbs sometimes, of course, but about 75 percent of them can be eliminated.

Wordy sentence: linking verb "is," 8 words total

Plant A **is** successful in terms of production.

Improved sentence: verb "produces," 4 words total

Plant A produces well.

Wordy phrase: linking verb "appears," 12 words total

There **appears** to be a tendency on the part of investment bankers...

Improved sentence: verb "tend, " 3 words total

Investment bankers tend...

Problem #2: Overused impersonal openings A frequent and related wordiness problem is the "impersonal opening." An *impersonal opening* is formed by a *to be* verb coupled with *it*, *there*, or *this*, resulting *in it is/it was*, *there is/there was*, or *this is/this was*. These six impersonal openings can usually be eliminated.

Wordy sentence: impersonal opening "It was," 7 words total

It was clear to the manager why...

Improved sentence: no impersonal opening, 4 words total

The manager knew why...

Wordy sentence: impersonal opening "There is, " 6 words total

There is no more space available.

Improved sentence: no impersonal opening, 5 words total

No more space is available.

Watch your prepositions. Overusing prepositions—words like *for*, *to*, and *of*, as listed on the facing page—produces wordy sentences.

Do not overuse prepositions Try circling, or having a computer program highlight, all the prepositions in a sample page of your writing. If you consistently find more than four in a sentence, you need to revise and shorten. *Of* is usually the worst offender.

Wordy sentence: 13 prepositions, 54 words total

> Central **to** our understanding **of** the problem **of** the organizational structure **in** the XYZ division **of** the ABC Company is the chain **of** command **between** the position **of** the division vice president and the subordinate departments, because although all **of** them are **under** this office, none **of** them is directly connected **up with** it.

Improved sentence: 3 prepositions, 24 words total

> The organizational problem **at** the ABC company's XYZ division is centered **in** the unclear connection **between** the division vice president and the subordinate departments.

Avoid compound prepositions In addition to overused prepositions, watch out for *compound prepositions*—that is, phrases with multiple prepositions—such as *in order to* instead of *to*. See the facing page.

Wordy sentence: 3 compound prepositions, 22 words total

> I am writing **in order to** list the potential issues **in regard to** the Russell account **in advance of** the client visit.

Improved sentence: zero compound prepositions, 16 words total

> I am writing **about** the Russell account **to** list the potential issues **before** the client visit.

Avoid elongated verbs with prepositions Finally, watch out for *elongated verbs*, sometimes called *smothered verbs*—that is, verbs that become unnecessarily elongated with prepositions.

Wordy sentence: verb with preposition, 11 words total

> We plan to **give consideration to** the idea at our meeting.

Improved sentence: verb alone, 9 words total

> We plan to **consider** the idea at our meeting.

EXAMPLES
WATCH YOUR PREPOSITIONS

1. Do not overuse prepositions.

after	by	near	to
as	for	of	under
at	from	on	until
before	in	over	up
between	like	through	with

2. Avoid compound prepositions.

Write	*Avoid compound prepositions*
about	in regard to, with reference to, in relation to, with regard to
because	due to the fact that, for the reason that, on the grounds that
before	in advance of, prior to, previous to
for	for the period of, for the purpose of
if	in the event that
near	in the proximity of
on	on the occasion of
to	in order to, for the purpose of, so as to, with a view toward
until	until such time as
when	at the point in time, at such time, as soon as
whether	the question as to whether
with	in connection with

3. Avoid elongated verbs with prepositions.

Write	*Avoid verb plus noun plus preposition*
analyze	perform an analysis of
assume	make assumptions about
can	be in a position to
conclude	reach a conclusion about
consider	give consideration to
decide	make a decision regarding
depends	is dependent on
examine	make an examination of
realize	come to the realization that
recommend	make a recommendation that
reduce	effect a reduction in
tend	exhibit a tendency to

2. Avoiding overlong sentences

Long, complicated sentences are harder to comprehend than shorter, simpler ones. How long is too long? One well-known readability formula recommends that sentences average 17 words. Other experts recommend 20 to 25 words. And most experts agree that you should cut sentences over 40 to 50 words. But writing is not like accounting: you cannot judge sentence length by any hard-and-fast rule. Rather, your sentence is too long anytime its length makes it confusing.

Watch out for two tendencies in particular: (1) too many main ideas in a sentence, usually signaled by using the word *and* more than once in a sentence, and (2) a hard-to-find main idea in a sentence, usually signaled by having too many piled-up phrases, parenthetical ideas, and qualifiers. If you tend to write overlong sentences, here are three solutions, moving from the least emphatic (paragraph form) to the most emphatic (bullet form).

Ineffective overlong sentence: 58 words

> Regardless of their seniority, all employees who hope to be promoted will continue their education either by enrolling in the special courses to be offered by the ABC Company, scheduled to be given on the next eight Saturdays, beginning on January 24, or by taking approved correspondence courses selected from a list available in the Staff Development Office.

Option 1: break into three sentences, using transitions

> Regardless of their seniority, all employees who hope to be promoted will continue their education in one of two ways. First, they may enroll in the special courses to be offered by the ABC Company, scheduled to be given on the next eight Saturdays, beginning on January 24. Second, they may take approved correspondence courses selected from a list available in the Staff Development Office.

Option 2: break up long sentence with internal enumeration

> Regardless of their seniority, all employees who hope to be promoted will continue their education in one of two ways: (1) they may enroll in the special courses to be offered by the ABC Company, scheduled to be given on the next eight Saturdays, beginning on January 24, or (2) they may take approved correspondence courses selected from a list available in the Staff Development Office.

Option 3: break up long sentence with bullet points

> Regardless of their seniority, all employees who hope to be promoted will continue their education in one of two ways:
>
> - They may enroll in the special courses to be offered by the ABC Company, scheduled to be given on the next eight Saturdays, beginning on January 24.
> - They may take approved correspondence courses selected from a list available in the Staff Development Office.

Good sentence length, however, is more subtle than merely limiting your sentences to a constant 20 to 25 words. Just because business writing avoids overlong sentences does not mean it should use short, choppy sentences, all of similar length. A lack of variety in sentence length or structure can be just as deadening as strings of long sentences, so watch out for monotonous, identically structured sentences. In addition, read your writing aloud to hear how your sentences sound; watch out for a deadly lack of rhythm or for sequences of words that no one would ever say.

II. CHOOSING A STYLE

MICROWRITING		
Section in this chapter:	**I. Editing for Brevity**	**II. Choosing a Style**
Goal:	To make writing concise	To make tone appropriate
Methods:	Avoiding wordiness Avoiding overlong sentences	Businesslike or bureaucratic? Active or passive? Jargon or no jargon?

Micro issues involved in editing for wordiness and sentence length differ significantly from issues of style. *Editing for brevity* is a cognitive and, to some extent, quantifiable skill. *Editing for style* requires more contextual sensitivity: it is bound up in your communication strategy—especially the context or culture in which you are communicating and your relationship with the reader.

Most of us have been taught to use, and have been rewarded for using, an academic style of writing. Sometimes that academic style is appropriate in business—for example, when you are writing to a group of engineers. Ineffective business writers, however, use the academic style automatically, instead of adjusting their style to the situation.

To choose an appropriate style, consider three sets of questions: (1) businesslike or bureaucratic word choice? (2) active or passive verbs? and (3) jargon or no jargon?

1. Businesslike or bureaucratic?

Think about your options and weigh the arguments before you choose a style to use in a given situation.

Understanding the differences Businesslike and bureaucratic styles are based on these kinds of differences:

Word and phrase length Business style uses short words and phrases, like those used in normal business conversation; bureaucratic style uses longer words and phrases.

Businesslike	*Bureaucratic*
about	pursuant to, in reference to
as you requested	pursuant to your request/our discussion
be aware	be cognizant of
get the facts	ascertain the data
here are	attached please find
if you need more help	should additional assistance be required
pay	remunerate
separately	under separate cover
until	pending determination of
use	utilize, utilization of

Pronouns and names Business style uses personal pronouns and refers to the reader and writer by name. Bureaucratic style avoids personal pronouns and avoids using the reader's and the writer's names.

Businesslike	*Bureaucratic*
I, you	one
me, reader's name	the undersigned, the aforenamed
I hope you will attend.	One would hope the vice president will attend.

Contractions Business style uses occasional contractions; bureaucratic style does not.

Businesslike	*Bureaucratic*
I won't be able to attend.	The vice president will be unable to attend.

Choosing a style There are arguments to be made for both styles.

Arguments for bureaucratic style (1) Formal phrases like "pending determination of" instead of "until" sound more important. (2) Formal phrases like "the aforementioned is attached" sound more traditional. (3) Cultural norms or audience expectations may require a bureaucratic style.

Arguments for business style (1) Bureaucratic phrases like "pending determination of" instead of "until" sound wordy and stilted. (2) Imitating the habits of business predecessors is about as sensible as writing with quill and ink instead of word processors. (3) Most business cultures and business audiences dislike stodgy, pompous, or convoluted writing styles.

Using business style If you choose to write in business style, read your writing aloud or imagine yourself saying it to someone. If you wouldn't say something because it sounds too stiff or formal, don't write it. Ask yourself, for example, if you would ever say to someone, "Per your request of today's date, enclosed please find the figures on the Nakano account." Instead, you would probably say, "Here are the figures on the Nakano account."

Naturally, however, you should not "write the way you talk" to the extent of becoming rambling, slangy, overly casual, and unorganized. Write the way you would talk at work. Writing expert John Fielden describes this business conversational style as follows: "it is simple; it is personal; it is warm without being syrupy; it is forceful, like a firm handshake."

2. Active or passive?

A second stylistic choice has to do with active or passive voice. The sentence *Paul decided* is active: the active agent (Paul) comes first, the active verb (decided) second. The sentence *It was decided by Paul* is passive: the passive verb (was decided) comes first, the active agent (Paul) second. Passive sentences always include or imply action done by someone or something. Both active voice and passive voice have advantages.

When to use active voice Use active voice when you want to avoid wordiness, avoid formality, place responsibility, and save your reader time.

Use active voice to avoid wordiness. Active sentences are usually shorter because they are less wordy.

Active: shorter

Paul decided.

Passive: longer

It was decided by Paul.

Use active voice to avoid formality. Active sentences usually sound less formal.

Active: less formal

Paul's evident bias made it hard for him to decide fairly.

Passive: more formal

A fair decision was rendered difficult by Paul's evident bias.

Use active voice to place responsibility. Active sentences make it easier for the reader to figure out who performed the action.

Active: clear who decided

Paul decided to undertake a special study.

Passive: unclear who decided

It has been decided that a special study be undertaken.

Use active voice to save the reader time. Perhaps most important, research shows that readers can process active sentences faster than passive sentences, in part because the active sentences are shorter and clearer. In the passive example that follows, the reader must pause momentarily and figure out who is making the statement.

Passive: slower for the reader to process

It is stated that...

Active: faster for the reader to process

The Tax Code states...

When to use passive voice Since passive sentences take longer for your reader to process, use them sparingly, only when you have good reason for doing so—to de-emphasize the writer, avoid responsibility, or make a transition.

Use passive voice to de-emphasize the writer. The passive allows writers to remove themselves from the sentence.

> *Active: emphasizes the writer*
>
> I recommend...
>
> *Passive: de-emphasizes the writer*
>
> It is recommended that...

Use passive voice to avoid responsibility. The passive allows writers to avoid placing responsibility on any one agent.

> *Active: places responsibility*
>
> I made a mistake.
>
> Lou Smith made a mistake.
>
> *Passive: avoids responsibility*
>
> A mistake was made.

Use passive voice occasionally for transition. Sometimes, using the passive allows you to place phrases appearing in two sentences close enough together so readers can grasp their connection more easily.

> *Active: does not connect the two sentences clearly*
>
> We will develop a list of tasks that will include all the projects. Each program manager will monitor his or her project.
>
> *Passive: "these projects" connects the two sentences more clearly*
>
> We will develop a list of tasks that will include all the projects. These projects will be monitored by each program manager.

When to use the imperative If you wish to use the active voice, but you don't want to keep repeating the word *I*, try using the imperative. Imperative sentences are those that start with a verb; the subject of the sentence, *you*, is implied. Use the imperative for these two reasons:

Use the imperative to avoid overuse of I. The imperative starts with a verb, not with *I*.

Not imperative: repeated use of I

I recommend that you improve quality control.

I recommend that you increase market share.

I recommend that you lower unit cost.

Imperative: avoids repeated I

Improve quality control.

Increase market share.

Lower unit cost.

Use the imperative to give clear instructions. Choose the imperative when you want to give clear instructions or recommendations without sounding harsh.

Not imperative: unclear who is supposed to do it

Quality control should be improved.

Not imperative: "you should" may sound harsh

You should improve quality control.

Imperative: gives clear instructions or recommendation

Improve quality control.

3. Jargon or no jargon?

A third stylistic consideration is how much and what kind of jargon is appropriate in any given situation.

What is jargon? Jargon is terminology associated with your field. Every profession has its jargon. Here are two examples, from the fields of economics and law.

Example: jargon from an economist

> The choice of exogenous variables in relation to multicollinearity is contingent upon the deviations of certain multiple coefficients.

Example: no jargon

> Supply determines demand.

Example: jargon from a lawyer

> This policy is used in consideration of the application therefor, copy of which application is attached hereto and made part hereof, and of the payment for said insurance on the life of the above-named insured.

Example: no jargon

> Here is your life insurance policy.

When to use jargon When you are writing to people within your field, jargon can be appropriate. Jargon is also appropriate when it serves as a shorthand that your reader understands for a complex idea or a commonly used lengthy term. Jargon is appropriate if it saves time and words without sacrificing understanding. For example, using acronyms such as EPS, LIFO, FIFO, IRR, and ROI to readers with the necessary accounting or finance backgrounds would certainly be appropriate. Finally, if you absolutely need to use jargon your audience may not understand, explain the acronym or phrase before you use it—for example, "internal rate of return (IRR)."

When to avoid jargon Avoid jargon if it is a ponderous and wordy way of saying something simple, rather than a short way of saying something complex—for example, *fiscal expenditures* instead of *cost, interface with* instead of *discuss*, or *render inoperative* instead of *stop.* In addition, avoid jargon if your reader doesn't understand it, may be confused by it, or might feel excluded by it.

This habit of using jargon with readers outside your field may be symptomatic of what former *Harvard Business Review* editor David Ewing calls "pathological professionalism." He asks: "Why do the perpetrators of these verbal monstrosities, knowing the material must be read and understood by innocent people, proceed with such sinister dedication? They rejoice in the difficulty of their trade. They find psychic rewards in producing esoteric and abstruse word combinations. They revel in the fact that only a small group, an elite counterculture, knows what in hell they are trying to say. Hence, the term *pathological professionalism*."

Chapters II, III, and IV (along with the appendices) have covered ideas for managerial writing—summarized on the checklists on the following two pages. The next three chapters will discuss managerial speaking skills.

MACROWRITING CHECKLIST
DOCUMENT- AND PARAGRAPH-LEVEL ISSUES

1. **Document design for "high skim value"**
   See pages 50–56.
   1. Are your headings and subheadings effective: stand-alone sense, parallel form, and limited wording?
   2. Do you use white space effectively: blocks of text, indentations, margins, and lists?
   3. Do you use typography effectively: consistent manner, readable font, limited use of capitals, readable size?

2. **Structural signposts for linkage**
   See pages 57–61.
   1. Do the ideas in your document link together—using back-and-forth references, section previews, and document design techniques?
   2. Does your opening build reader interest, explain your purpose for writing, and provide a preview? Does your closing summarize or include action steps?

3. **Effective paragraphs or sections**
   See pages 62–65.
   1. Does each paragraph or section have a generalization (topic sentence or heading), followed by support for that generalization?
   2. Do you use structural signposts to link ideas within each paragraph or section?

MICROWRITING CHECKLIST SENTENCE- AND WORD-LEVEL ISSUES
1. Brevity: Is your writing concise? See pages 68–73. 1. Do you avoid wordiness (overuse of prepositions and linking verbs)? 2. Do you avoid overlong sentences?
2. Style: Is your tone appropriate? See pages 74–81. Have you chosen an appropriate tone: businesslike or bureaucratic? Active or passive? Jargon or no jargon?
3. Format: Have you used business formats? See pages 162–169. Have you used memo, letter, or report formats effectively?
4. Correctness See pages 173–184. Have you used correct grammar and punctuation?

CHAPTER V OUTLINE

I. Tell/sell presentations
   1. Structuring a presentation
   2. Working from an outline

II. Questions and answers

III. Consult/join meetings
   1. Preparation before the meeting
   2. Participation during the meeting
   3. Decision-making and follow-up

IV. Special speaking situations

CHAPTER V

Speaking: Verbal Structure

In this chapter, we consider the verbal aspect of speaking—how to structure what you say in various group speaking situations. In Chapters VI and VII, we will look at the two other aspects of presentations: visual aids and nonverbal delivery skills.

How you structure what you say depends on the situation in which you are speaking. The chart that follows illustrates the three kinds of group speaking situations covered in this chapter: (1) tell/sell presentations, (2) questions and answers, and (3) consult/join meetings. This chapter also includes tips for special speaking situations.

SPEAKING: VERBAL STRUCTURE			
Section in this chapter:	**I. Tell/Sell Presentations**	**II. Questions and Answers**	**III. Consult/Join Meetings**
Who speaks most:	You	You to audience	You and audience
Possible purposes:	To inform or to persuade	To answer questions	To discuss or to decide

I. TELL/SELL PRESENTATIONS

SPEAKING: VERBAL STRUCTURE			
Section in this chapter:	**I. Tell/Sell Presentations**	**II. Questions and Answers**	**III. Consult/Join Meetings**
Who speaks most:	You	You to audience	You and audience
Possible purposes:	To inform or to persuade	To answer questions	To discuss or to decide

1. Preparing "what to say"

If you are speaking to a group of people primarily to inform or persuade them, use these techniques to structure what you say. Remember that presenting information orally differs from presenting it in writing. An effective presentation structure includes (1) an opening, (2) a preview of the main points, (3) clearly demarcated main points, and (4) a closing.

Use an effective opening. Openings are important in all forms of communication, as we discussed with the Audience Memory Curve on page 19. When you make an oral presentation, however, your opening is even more crucial than it is when you write. Unlike your readers, who decide when and where to read your document, your listeners have had the time and place imposed on them; they are likely to have other things on their minds. Therefore, always use the first minute or so of your presentation for your opening, what many experts call a "grabber."

To decide what to say during your opening or "grabber," think about the audience and context in which you will be speaking. Is their interest level low or high? Do they know you well or not? Is it obvious how the topic relates to them or not? Given your audience analysis, choose from among the following techniques:

- *Arouse their interest.* Some techniques to arouse their interest and pique their curiosity include a rhetorical question, a promise of what your presentation will deliver, a vivid image, a startling example or story, an alarming statistic, a quotation, a projection into the future, or a personal story that makes a business point.

- *Show how the topic relates to them.* Another possibility is to open your presentation by referring to something familiar to your audience, something they can easily relate to. Examples of this kind of opening include a reference to your audience (who they are), to the occasion (why you are there), to the relationship between the audience and the subject, or to someone or something familiar to the audience.
- *Show "what's in it for them."* If it's not clear how they would benefit from your presentation, review the audience motivation techniques discussed on pages 15–17 for possible use in your opening.
- *Establish your credibility.* If your audience doesn't know you, introduce yourself and review the credibility factors discussed on pages 8–9 for possible use in your opening, especially the possibility of emphasizing the "common ground."
- *Be careful using humor.* When many people think of a presentation opening, they think of telling a joke. Actually, you don't necessarily have to be humorous or entertaining in your opening. Use humor only if it fits your personality and style, if it is appropriate for every member of the audience, and if it relates to the specific topic or occasion. Never use humor that might make anyone feel left out, put down, or trivialized.

Next, give a preview. A preview is a table of contents, an agenda, an outline of what you will be covering in your presentation. Think about the contrast between listeners and readers. Your readers can skim a document, see how long it is, and read your headings and subheadings before they start reading. Your listeners, by contrast, have no idea what you will be covering unless you tell them. One of the most common problems in business presentations is the lack of a preview. Always give an explicit preview before you begin discussing your main points; it will help your audience understand and remember what you say.

In the most formal situations, a preview might sound like this: "In the next twenty minutes, I will discuss sales in each of three regions: the Southeast, the Far West, and the Midwest." On less formal occasions, your preview might be "I'd like to go over the sales figures in three regions." In any situation, the point of the preview is to give your audience a skeleton view, a very general outline, of what you will be discussing.

State your main points clearly On pages 38–39, we discussed how to organize material clearly. In addition to those general organizational principles, here are three specific techniques to apply to oral presentation structure.

Limit your main points Be sure to limit the number of main points you make in a presentation, since listeners cannot process as much information as readers can. Experiments in cognitive psychology show that people cannot easily comprehend more than five to seven main points. Naturally, this doesn't mean that you say five things and sit down; it means that you should group your complex ideas into five to seven major areas.

Use explicit transitions When you are speaking, you need longer, more explicit transitions between major sections or subsections than when you are writing. Listeners do not stay oriented as easily as readers do; they may not remember what you are listing. Instead of using short transitions like "second," use longer transitions, such as "the second recommendation is" or "Let's move on to the second recommendation."

Provide internal summaries Finally, use internal summaries to conclude each major section or subsection. Listeners may not remember information they hear only once. Here is an example of an internal summary followed by an explicit transition to the next main section: "Now that we have looked at the three elements of the marketing plan—modifying the promotion program, increasing direct mail, and eliminating the coupon program—let's turn to the financial implications of this plan."

Keep their interest high In addition to delivering a clear and rational message, remember to keep your audience's attention with an emotionally appealing message. Again, your audience analysis will drive how much emotion is appropriate, but most business presenters underestimate the importance of emotion. For example, research shows that stories and case illustrations have more impact than only statistical data. Think about dynamism, interest, and fun in addition to organization, details, and information. Think about incorporating audience members' names; for example, instead of "when two departments fill out this form," say "when Jose in accounting and Joe in human resources fill out this form."

Use an effective closing Your audience is likely to remember your last words. So don't waste your closing saying something like "Well, that's all I have to say" or "I guess that's about it." Also, don't confuse your audience by introducing a completely new topic.

Instead, use a strong, obvious transitional phrase—such as "to summarize" or "in conclusion"—to introduce your closing remarks. Here are some options for effective closings:

- *Give a summary.* One effective closing is to summarize your main points. You may feel as though you're being repetitive, but this kind of reinforcement is extremely effective when you are explaining or instructing.
- *Arouse their enthusiasm.* Another possibility is to close with a quote, an appeal, or a challenge.
- *Refer to the opening.* A third kind of closing is to refer to the rhetorical question, promise, image, or story you used in your opening.
- *End with the action steps.* You might choose to end with a call to action based on what you have presented, making the "what next?" step explicit. Emphasize "what's in it for them" if they take these action steps.

2. Working from an outline

Another aspect of structuring a presentation has to do with the form your notes take. Businesspeople don't have the time to memorize every presentation they make; very few business speakers must read speeches word for word. (If you do, however, see pages 104–105 on manuscript speeches.) At the same time, business audiences expect eye contact and speaker interaction, so instead of memorizing or reading, work from an outline.

Advantages of outlines With an outline, you know you can refer to notes if necessary. However, you will avoid both the overreliance on notes caused by word-for-word manuscripts and the terror of speaking with no notes at all. You can also add notes to yourself (e.g., "Stand straight!" or "Show line chart here").

How to outline The purpose of your outline is to jog your memory; the outline is not a manuscript. You want to spend most of your time during the presentation looking at the audience, not reading. Therefore, do not write out complete sentences; instead, print very short phrases for each point or subpoint. Leave lots of white space. Use big enough lettering so that you can read your notes at arm's length.

Cards versus paper Most experts suggest writing your outline on 5-by-7- or 4-by-6-inch cards, either handwritten or printed from a computer using a large font. Cards are easier to hold and carry if you want to move to your visual aid or elsewhere; they allow you to add to, subtract from, or rearrange your material easily; they help some people force themselves to outline phrases rather than writing complete sentences. Each notecard should contain about five minutes' worth of information. Some speakers prefer using regular-sized paper for their outline, because they can usually put their paper down on a table, desk, or lectern. Use the method that feels more comfortable and looks less awkward for you.

Structuring your presentation in outline form is one of the three basic components of a tell/sell presentation. The second component is composing and using tell/sell visual aids, explained on pages 109–138; the third is improving nonverbal delivery, explained on pages 143–155.

II. QUESTION AND ANSWERS

SPEAKING: VERBAL STRUCTURE			
Section in this chapter:	**I. Tell/Sell Presentations**	**II. Questions and Answers**	**III. Consult/Join Meetings**
Who speaks most:	You	You to audience	You and audience
Possible purposes:	To inform or to persuade	To answer questions	To discuss or to decide

Most presentations involve interaction between the speaker and the audience in the form of questions and answers. Dealing effectively with questions and answers involves deciding when to take questions, how to take questions, what to say if you don't know the answer, and how to answer difficult questions.

When to take questions Well before the presentation, think about when you will take questions. Then be sure to inform your audience at the beginning of the presentation. Say, for example, "Please feel free to ask questions as they come up" or "Please hold all your questions until the end of the presentation" or "Feel free to interrupt with questions of understanding or clarification, but since we only have an hour together, please hold questions of debate or discussion until the end."

Usually, audience and cultural expectations are fairly clear: the current trend in most Anglo-American business presentations is to include questions during the presentation; sometimes, however, the norm is for a question-and-answer period at the end of the presentation. If the choice is up to you, think about the following advantages and disadvantages.

Questions after the presentation If you take questions after the presentation, you will maintain control over the schedule and the flow of information. However, you risk (1) losing your audience's attention and perhaps even comprehension if they cannot interrupt with their questions, and (2) placing yourself in an awkward position if important audience members interrupt with questions after you've asked them not to. Since audiences tend to remember more material from the beginning and the end of a presentation, however, having "Q&A" last places undue emphasis on the question period. To alleviate this problem, save time for a two- to three-minute summary after the question period.

Questions during the presentation If you take questions during the presentation, the questions will be more meaningful to the questioner, the feedback will be more immediate, and your audience may listen more actively. However, questions during the presentation can upset your schedule and waste time. To alleviate these problems, (1) allow enough time for questions and (2) control digressions.

How to take questions Once you've established when to take questions, prepare yourself for how you will take them.

Prepare in advance Prepare yourself by anticipating possible questions. Try to guess what the questions will be. Bring along extra information, perhaps even extra visual aids, to answer such questions if they come up. Another way to anticipate questions is to ask a colleague to play devil's advocate during your rehearsal.

As you prepare, try to control your attitude toward the process. Instead of going in with a defensive attitude, think of it as a compliment if your listeners are interested enough to ask for clarification, amplification, or justification.

Frequently asked questions include those of (1) value ("Are you sure we really need this?" or "What will happen if we don't do this?"), (2) cost ("Can we do it for less?"), (3) action ("How can we do it?" or "Will this action cause new problems?"), and (4) details ("What is your source?" or "Is that number correct?").

Show your understanding When someone asks a question, listen carefully to be sure you understand it before you answer. Paraphrase or summarize complicated questions to make sure you're on the right track. If the group is large, paraphrase or repeat all questions to be sure everyone in the audience hears them. If someone asks a question you don't understand, say something like "Could you restate that? I'm afraid I don't understand the question," not "Your question isn't clear."

Stick to your objective and your organization Answer the question, but always keep your communication objective in mind. Even if you have a lot of information for your answer, limit yourself to whatever advances your objective. Don't go off on rambling tangents. If necessary, divert the question back to your main ideas. If someone asks a question you had planned to cover later in your talk, try to answer it in a nutshell and then make it clear that you will cover it in more detail later.

Keep everyone involved Keep the entire audience involved by calling on people from various locations in the audience and by avoiding a one-to-one conversation with a single member of the audience. When you answer, maintain eye contact with the entire audience, not just with the person who asked the question. Also, avoid ending your answer by looking right at the questioner: he or she may feel invited to ask another question.

What to say if you don't know the answer Sometimes you absolutely don't know the answer; sometimes you don't know the answer without some time to gather your thoughts.

If you don't know If you don't know the answer, say, "I don't know." Even better, suggest where the person might find the answer. Better still, offer to get the answer yourself. For example, "Off the top of my head, I don't know the sales figures for that region, but I'll look them up and have them on your desk by tomorrow morning." Never hazard a guess unless you make it extremely clear that it is only a guess.

If you need some time to think If you are momentarily stymied by a question, here are some techniques to buy you some thinking time: (1) Repeat: "You're wondering how to deal with this situation." (2) Turn the question around: "How would *you* deal with this situation?" (3) Turn the question outward: "How would the rest of you deal with this situation?" (4) Reflect: "Good question. Let's think about that for a moment." (5) Write: If you are using a suitable visual aid, write down the main point of the question as you think.

How to answer difficult questions Some questions are especially challenging because they are confusing, controlling, or hostile.

Confusing questions Confusing questions may be long, rambling, multifaceted, or overly global. In these cases, paraphrase the question before you answer, refocusing to make it appropriate for your communication objective. If the questioner repeats the inappropriately long version of the question, say "I wish we had more time so we could discuss that" or "Let's explore that in more detail after the presentation is over."

Controlling questions Some questions are not really questions; they are statements. In the case of these mini-lectures, do not feel obliged to answer or to ask "So what exactly is your question?" Instead, thank them for their comments, perhaps even paraphrasing their ideas, and then proceed with your presentation.

Other controlling questions are those questions the audience member clearly wants to answer him- or herself or that focus on his or her interests only. In these cases, you need to decide whether you want to (1) regain control yourself by refocusing on your communication objective or (2) change your focus midstream by turning the question back to them ("What do you think we ought to do?"). For example, if you were explaining a new procedure to a large group of employees, you would probably opt to regain control; if you were talking to a small group of important clients, you would probably choose to change focus to meet their needs.

Hostile questions People may be hostile because of lack of information; in these cases, you can influence them through facts and logic. Many times, however, they may be hostile because they feel passionate, threatened, defensive, isolated, or resentful of authority or change. Faced with a hostile question, take a deep breath, identify the hostility ("I understand you feel upset about this"), and answer the question nonemotionally and nonpersonally. Sometimes, you may be able to find a common ground ("We're both trying to do what we feel is in the customer's best interest"). Sometimes, however, you have no choice but to agree to disagree, paraphrasing both points of view clearly.

III. CONSULT/JOIN MEETINGS

SPEAKING: VERBAL STRUCTURE			
Section in this chapter:	**I. Tell/Sell Presentations**	**II. Questions and Answers**	**III. Consult/Join Meetings**
Who speaks most:	You	You to audience	You and audience
Possible purposes:	To inform or to persuade	To answer questions	To discuss or to decide

A third kind of verbal structure is that used when you are not presenting information (that is, in tell/sell situations) but rather when you are eliciting information from others (that is, in consult/join situations). In reality, we all know that some meetings include presentations and reports and that some presentations turn into free-for-all discussions. However, for the purposes of explaining interactive versus presentational skills, let's assume that in a meeting you are trying to elicit group feedback rather than to present your own ideas.

Many businesspeople erroneously assume that running a meeting is easy, simple, and straightforward. Actually, meetings involve a complex and difficult set of tasks. According to negotiation expert Lindsay Rahmun, meetings are difficult because of a set of inherent contradictions she dubs "the participant's dilemma": we expect people to be thoughtful and innovative, yet simultaneously fast and efficient; we are annoyed when people don't participate, yet annoyed when they talk too much; we expect people to offer their best ideas, yet not get defensive when those ideas are modified or rejected; we want to hold high standards of quality and resist "groupthink," yet at the same time we call people stubborn and inflexible if they don't move with the group; we want to work with a small group for efficiency, yet with a large group for inclusiveness.

Following are some guidelines for dealing with the complex set of issues of (1) preparation before the meeting, (2) participation during the meeting, and (3) decision-making and follow-up after the meeting.

I. Preparation before the meeting

Before the meeting, think carefully about the meeting objective, participants, agenda, and roles.

Set the objective The next time you are thinking about calling a meeting, ask yourself, "Is the meeting necessary?" Perhaps the single most prevalent complaint about meetings is that they are called unnecessarily. A good way to start is to state your meeting objective specifically: "As a result of this meeting, we will accomplish _______." Meetings should be reserved for situations in which you need group idea generation, discussion, feedback, and decision-making, and/or when you are trying to build group identity, relationships, and trust. Meetings should not be for routine announcements or for presenting your own finalized ideas.

Select the participants Here are two considerations for selecting participants: (1) Think about the subgroups that must be represented; at the same time, remember that it's difficult to reach a consensus with more than about eight participants. (2) Consider the hierarchical levels of participants. In general, if you want to make decisions and avoid posturing and jockeying, do not include more than two hierarchical levels of participants.

Set the agenda Since the whole purpose of a meeting to is elicit information from other people, prepare your agenda carefully and in advance, so that participants can think of ideas in advance.

- *State the objective*. Define the meeting objective or meeting impetus as specifically as possible, so that participants will have no doubt about it; state the purpose clearly on the agenda, and restate it at the beginning of the meeting.

- *Schedule agenda items*. As you set your agenda, think about the meeting length and order of items. Productivity tends to drop after about two hours or if you have too many topics to cover. Schedule a series of short meetings if the agenda requires more time. Deal with long reports by asking presenters to hand in a written report for the sake of the record, but to report verbally the most important items or the items on which they want group response. Decide where you want to schedule sensitive topics on the agenda. You can save sensitive topics for the end if you think opening with major disagreements might keep the meeting from proceeding effectively. Alternatively, you can start with the most important topic, even if it is sensitive, to allow sufficient time to deal with the important topic and if you fear that people won't focus on the first items if they know a big controversy is coming up.
- *State the purpose for each agenda item*. Then, for each item on the agenda, answer the following questions for the participants: (1) What is the purpose of each agenda item? Clearly differentiate items that are "for your information," "for discussion," or "for a decision." (2) What is your tentative timing for each topic? (3) Who is in charge of each item? Will you have various presenters or will you run the whole meeting yourself? (4) How should they prepare? Don't waste time lecturing during the meeting itself; instead, include sufficient background information with the agenda.
- *Clarify group preparation*. Let participants know how they should prepare and how they will be expected to contribute. Don't put people on the spot in the meeting. Instead, let them know in advance what will be expected of them—for example, "Think about the pros and cons of this proposal" or "List five ideas before the meeting."
- *Distribute the agenda in advance*. If you want to elicit ideas from people, give them time to think about the agenda items before the meeting. For a complicated financial or analytic agenda, distribute the agenda about a week in advance; for a regular agenda, distribute it a couple of days in advance.

2. Participation during the meeting

Here are some techniques to increase participation at a meeting.

Delegating tasks Your first task is to decide what role(s) you are going to perform yourself—and which you will delegate to someone else.

- *Facilitator:* If you have strong feelings about the subject at hand or want to participate actively, you should consider asking someone else to facilitate the discussion. If you choose to facilitate it yourself, you must refrain from dominating the discussion: it's difficult to listen to others' points of view when you are trying to convince them of your own.
- *Timer:* You may wish to appoint someone else to serve as timekeeper, because it's hard to concentrate on the discussion and keep your mind on the time all at once. Going over the time limit, running off on tangents, and losing control of time can be big problems; conversely, controlling the flow too much and cutting people off can also be problems. Think about how you are going to deal with time issues, and, within reason, stick to your decision or group contract on timing.
- *Minutes writer:* You may also want to appoint someone else to write up minutes after the meeting, to check the minutes before they are distributed, and to decide who will receive a copy of the minutes.
- *Scribe:* Finally, instead of choosing to record participant comments during the meeting yourself, consider asking someone else to serve as scribe. This increasingly popular technique offers three benefits. (1) *Enhances facilitation:* Managing the discussion will be much easier for you, because you don't have to talk and write at the same time. (2) *Improves legibility:* The scribe can write more carefully and you can select someone with neat handwriting. (3) *Saves time:* Perhaps most important, using a scribe saves time, because you can go on to discuss the next point while the scribe is still recording the previous point.

  However, determining what to record and when to record it is a tool of control and influence, so if you use someone else as scribe, make it extremely clear in advance how you will work together. You may, for example, want to specify that the scribe records only the specific wording you signal to him or her to write down during the session; or you may empower the scribe to record at his or her discretion. Another technique is to use two scribes to take turns recording ideas if you think ideas will be flowing fast.

Opening the meeting At the beginning of the meeting, plan to do the following:

- *Set the tone.* Start on time. Get people interested, involved, and enthusiastic by giving a short introduction and then involving them early.
- *Explain the agenda.* Make sure everyone understands and agrees on the meeting's purpose, impetus, agenda, and decision-making technique. Sometimes, you may wish to open the meeting by modifying the agenda or adding discussion items with the group.
- *Get people to agree on ground rules.* Meetings will run much more effectively if everyone agrees explicitly on the ground rules at the outset. If you wait until someone has erred before you clarify the rules, the person will feel humiliated. If, however, you have the rules clear from the start, a brief reminder will usually work. You can either work together with the group to set up ground rules or list the ground rules in advance yourself. You might even consider posting the ground rules on the wall. Examples of ground rules include the following: We will start and stop on time. We will not interrupt. We will stick to the agenda. We will show respect for one another and not engage in personal attacks. We will treat all information as confidential.
- *Involve people early.* The earlier you can get participants involved in some way, the more likely they are to participate. If you are dealing with a passive or quiet group, you might think of some activity or icebreaker that involves them early in the session.

During the meeting Throughout the meeting, use the following skills to encourage everybody's participation.

- *Use good listening skills.* Use the listening skills discussed on pages 156–159, especially (1) asking open-ended questions that cannot be answered "yes" or "no," such as "What are your reactions to this proposal?" (2) paraphrasing participant responses by restating them verbally and in writing on charts; and (3) modeling "attending skills" that give physical attention to the speaker through effective body language.
- *Show support for every person's right to speak.* Support does not necessarily mean agreement. Instead, showing support means you hear and acknowledge each idea. In fact, you may very well end up hearing contradictory ideas. That is perfectly appropriate in a meeting; you can go back and evaluate the ideas after they are all out on the table. Responses to show support include "That idea shows a lot of thought. What do the rest of you think?" and "Let's consider what Kim has just recommended." Responses that do not show support include "I disagree," "That's wrong because. . . ," or and "That won't work, because. . . ." Finally, encourage discussion of ideas, not of personalities.
- *Avoid dominance by any one person or subgroup.* Here are some techniques to avoid letting any one person or group dominate the discussion: (1) Draw in each person giving him or her a chance to speak to the issue, or say something along the lines of "Let's hear from those who haven't spoken yet"—but don't put them on the spot by calling on them by name. (2) Use a firm but tactful reminder of the ground rules, such as "Wait, Chris. Remember, we agreed on no interrupting" or "Excuse me, Darcy, but we need to keep our remarks brief so everyone has the chance to talk." (3) Talk to disruptive, very verbal, or high-status people privately before or after the meeting to avoid a direct confrontation in front of the group. Try to understand them and enlist their help in making the next meeting more productive. (4) Use nonverbal methods—such as turning your body toward the person who is being interrupted or raising your hand in a "wait a minute" gesture to the person who is interrupting. (5) Sit next to disrupters, rather than across from them, so they can't catch your eye as easily. (6) Give the disrupter a job to do—keep the minutes or chair a subcommittee. Often, these people are looking for some kind of status or recognition.

- *Explain your ideas.* If you have decided that it is appropriate for the facilitator to participate in the discussion, explain your own ideas quickly. Unless you are giving a formal report during the meeting, you usually won't talk for more than a few minutes at a time. Speak only when it is appropriate. Stick to the agenda; avoid extraneous ideas. Don't bring up ideas at an inappropriate time during a meeting; for example, don't start questioning the solution all over again after the group has already decided to implement it.
- *Relate to others.* Relate to others' ideas rather than grandstanding your own. If you agree with others, you might supply supporting material such as examples, statistics, or applications of the idea. If you disagree, state your disagreements carefully by disagreeing with ideas—not with people personally. Say, for example, "That project may be very time consuming" instead of "The project Elizabeth has proposed will take too long!" Say "I don't understand that wording" instead of "Darcy's sentence doesn't make any sense." Disagree by saying "I'm not comfortable with..." or "What concerns me about your ideas..." instead of "I disagree with..." or "That won't work because...."
- *Don't talk too much.* It is hard to avoid dominating a meeting you are running. To control yourself, avoid interrupting, arguing, criticizing, or overdefending; don't talk for more than a couple of minutes; ask other people to contribute; ask someone else to present background information; ask questions instead of answering them; talk with them, not to them. You have decided to call a meeting; therefore, don't deliver a lecture or presentation.

3. Decision-making and follow-up

Don't waste all the valuable ideas you have gained from the meeting participants; use the following techniques to make a decision and to follow up.

Decision-making Some items on your agenda may require a decision. Choose, or have the group choose, how decisions will be made—and make it clear to the participants in advance which method you plan to use. Keep in mind that decision-making methods vary in different organizations and cultures.

- *By one person or majority vote* These two methods are quite fast; they are effective when the decision is not particularly important to everyone in the group or when there are severe time constraints. The disadvantage of these methods, however, is that some people may feel left out, ignored, or defeated—and these people may later sabotage the implementation. On the other hand, most people do not mind serving in an advisory board capacity only, as long as you make it clear to them in advance.
- *By consensus* Consensus means reaching a compromise that may not be everybody's first choice but that each person is willing to agree on and implement. Consensus involves hearing all points of view and incorporating these viewpoints into the solution, so it is time consuming and requires group commitment to the process. Unlike majority rule, consensus is reached by discussion, not by a vote. For example, the facilitator might ask "Do you all feel comfortable with this solution?" or "Seems to me we've reached consensus around this idea. Am I right?" Consensus does not mean unanimity; no participant has veto power. If one person seems to be the lone holdout for a position, say something like "Well, Fran, we understand your point clearly, but the rest of us don't want that solution. Can you live with this one instead?"

Follow-up How you end the meeting can be the most crucial key to success: all the time and effort spent on the meeting itself will be wasted if no one acts upon the ideas. At the close of the meeting, gauge the mood of the group: if issues are still unresolved, consider the need for further discussion; if issues have been resolved, don't rest on your laurels. Even if you feel bored, tired, and eager to get out of the room, or excited, exhilarated, and eager to celebrate, take the time to figure out how you are going to follow up with a permanent record and an action plan.

- *Permanent record* Most meetings should be documented with a permanent record of some kind, usually called the "minutes," to record what occurred and to communicate those results. The nature of the minutes will vary with the meeting's purpose; ineffective minutes are either too detailed or too general; effective minutes include the issues discussed, the alternatives considered, the decisions reached, and the action plan. You can write the minutes yourself, appoint someone else at the beginning of the meeting, or use the electronic methods discussed previously. Eventually, participants should receive hard or electronic copy of the minutes and the action plan.
- *Action plan* The group should agree to an action plan, to include (1) what actions are to be taken, (2) who is responsible for each action, (3) the timeframe for each action, and (4) how the action will be reported back to the group. A good way to start your next meeting might be to present an update on the previous meeting's action plan.

IV. SPECIAL SPEAKING SITUATIONS

In addition to the three standard speaking situations already covered in this chapter, you may find yourself in other kinds of situations. This section offers some additional techniques for dealing with (1) manuscript speaking, (2) impromptu speaking, (3) team presentations, and (4) media and telecommunications.

Manuscript speaking The tell/sell presentations discussed in the first section of this chapter are prepared, but not read word for word. You may find, however, that you are occasionally called upon to speak word for word from a manuscript.

Use "spoken style" The main problem people have in writing manuscript speeches is that they use "written style" instead of "spoken style." A speech in written style may look fine on paper, but when delivered, it sounds stilted, formal, and pompous. When you write a manuscript speech, then, keep in mind four aspects of spoken style: (1) Avoid phrases no one would actually say, phrases that sound stilted or are hard to pronounce. For example, you might write, "If you were asked to do so," but you would say, "If someone asked you to do that." (2) Avoid phrases separating the subject from the verb. Your reader can easily follow this sentence: "Linda Argenti, who is currently the president of ABC Company, will be the first speaker on the panel." You make it much easier for the listener, however, if you do not separate the subject from the verb: "President Linda Argenti will be the first speaker on the panel." (3) Use shorter sentences. Speech writing generally uses shorter sentences and sometimes even sentence fragments. (4) Remember that rhythm is much more important in spoken style than in written style. Consider, for example, the rhythmic impact of Patrick Henry's famous quotation "Give me liberty or give me death." Similarly, John Kennedy's rhythmic "Ask not what your country can do for you; ask what you can do for your country" is more effective than the unrhythmic "Don't ask what your country can do for you, but what you can do for it."

Write and edit Keeping the preceding four considerations in mind, write the first draft of your speech, or write notes and then record yourself speaking from those notes. The transcript of what you just recorded becomes the draft of the speech. Once you have a draft, edit it and then read it aloud (or have the person for whom you're writing the speech read it aloud). After making any necessary changes, you are ready to type the manuscript in its final form.

Prepare the manuscript A speech manuscript looks different from a regular page of writing. For one thing, it should be typed in a large font. The margins also look strange: leave about one third of the right side of the page blank for notes; leave about one third at the bottom of the page blank so that your head will not drop too low as you read. Since it is awkward to read a sentence that starts on one page and finishes on the next, never break a sentence between two pages. In fact, many speech experts suggest never breaking even a paragraph between two pages. Never staple the pages of a speech; the speaker should be able to slide the page to one side. Finally, many speakers underline key words for vocal emphasis.

Impromptu speaking When you speak on an impromptu basis, you talk on the spur of the moment, without advance preparation. For example, your boss may suddenly ask you to "bring us up to date on a certain service." Usually, of course, you will not be asked to make impromptu remarks unless you have some knowledge in the area.

Here are some suggestions to help you in impromptu speaking situations: (1) Anticipate. Try to avoid truly impromptu situations. Guess at the probability of your being called on during discussions, meetings, or interviews. Guess at the topics you might be asked to discuss. (2) Keep your remarks short. Say what you have to say and then stop. Do not ramble on, feeling that you must deliver a lengthy lecture. (3) Organize as well as you can. If you have a few seconds, jot down your main points. Stick to them; avoid tangents. (4) Relate to experience. You will speak more easily and confidently if you try to relate the topic to your specific experiences and to the topics you know best.

Team presentations Make sure your team presentations are organized, unified, and coherent—not simply an unrelated series of individual presentations.

Organize as a whole The major problem with team presentations occurs when each presenter prepares a separate part, and the parts never coalesce into a coherent whole. To avoid this problem, structure your presentation agenda by content areas, not by the number of team members. After your team decides on a presentation agenda, decide who will speak when; one speaker may cover two content sections, or one content section may be covered by multiple speakers.

Provide content transitions between speakers To begin, one team member should provide the opening and preview for the presentation as a whole, introducing the team members and the topics they will cover. (See pages 86–87.) Between each speaker, provide an internal summary ("Now that I have explained our proposal") and a content link to the next section ("Karla will show you the financial implications of the proposal").

Use visual aids consistently Your visuals should look alike: use the same graphic software, template, and color coding (e.g., blue for all the main headings throughout). (See pages 109–131.) Your use of visuals should also be consistent in the way you use assistance from one another, pile your slides, meter information, use the remote versus computer keys, and so forth. (See pages 136–138.)

Rehearse and deliver as a group In your first run-through—or what speaking expert Antony Jay calls the "stagger-through"—practice what you will say, the exact wording of your transitions, rough drafts of your visuals, and decide where team members will sit while others speak. In a second run-through, work to perfect your delivery and flow. During the presentation, remember that every member of the team is always "on stage" to the audience, from the moment you walk in the room; therefore, be sure to look fully attentive when other group members are speaking.

Answer questions consistently Decide beforehand how you will handle questions and answers, including such issues as who will serve as moderator to direct questions and whether you will stand or sit to answer questions. (See pages 91–94 for more on questions.)

Media and telecommunications Here are three sets of suggestions for dealing with speaking situations involving media and telecommunications.

Preparing in advance Gather your data in advance: get together any reports, correspondence, and notes you will need for reference. Also, jot down a brief outline of the points you want to cover. This will help you avoid rambling and forgetting important points or questions. If you are appearing on television or radio, anticipate questions you may be asked. Just as important, prepare the main points you want to emphasize.

Using audio devices Audio devices include telephones and microphones (for radio, television, video, or videoteleconferencing). (1) Speak conversationally, using pauses and inflection, as though you were addressing a small group of people. (2) Watch your volume and distance: omnidirectional microphones will pick up sounds equally from all directions; for unidirectional microphones, you must keep your distance (which can vary from 2 to 20 inches) constant. (3) Avoid unwanted sounds: breathe quietly; avoid rattling your paper, drumming your fingers, scraping your chair, and jingling coins.

Being on camera You will work with a camera when you are speaking on video, videoteleconference, or television. (1) Prepare for mechanical distractions. Rehearse on the set to learn cues and see the equipment. (2) Decide where to focus: at the camera, at the interviewer, or at the other people present. If you are recording a one-person video, you will probably look directly at the camera; if you are appearing on a talk show, you will probably look at the host; if you are appearing on a videoteleconference, you will probably look at the other participants. (3) Dress appropriately. In general, dress unobtrusively, especially if you are appearing on television. Generally, that means solid colors like gray, blue, and beige. Avoid tweeds, stripes, and patterns that will appear to jump around on the screen. Avoid white, which may glare, and black, which absorbs light. Other than a watch or a wedding ring, avoid jewelry, especially if it is jangling or otherwise distracting.

Besides verbal structure (covered in this chapter), think about visual aids (Chapter 6) and nonverbal delivery (Chapter 7.)

CHAPTER VI OUTLINE

I. Designing the presentation as a whole
   1. Listing your main ideas on an agenda chart
   2. Providing evidence on "back-up" charts
   3. Using "message titles" and "stand-alone sense"
   4. Providing transitions between each visual

II. Designing each individual chart
   1. Designing graphs to show quantitative data
   2. Designing diagrams to show nonquantitative concepts
   3. Designing word charts to show main ideas
   4. Using typography effectively
   5. Using color effectively
   6. Editing each chart

III. Choosing visual aid equipment

IV. Using visual aids effectively

CHAPTER VI

Speaking: Visual Aids

No matter how well you have prepared what you are going to say (Chapter V) or how skilled you may be in your nonverbal speaking delivery (Chapter VII), your audience still has the capacity to daydream: they can think faster than you can speak. To keep them concentrating on your ideas, provide visual aids that back up what you're saying. Visual aids increase your audience's comprehension and retention; add interest, variety, and impact; and remain in the memory longer than words.

Here are some techniques to use for (1) designing the visual presentation as a whole, (2) designing each individual chart, (3) choosing the equipment, and (4) using visuals effectively.

VISUAL AIDS			
I. Designing the presentation as a whole	II. Designing each individual chart	III. Choosing visual aid equipment	IV. Using visual aids effectively

I. DESIGNING THE PRESENTATION AS A WHOLE

VISUAL AIDS			
I. Designing the presentation as a whole	II. Designing each individual chart	III. Choosing visual aid equipment	IV. Using visual aids effectively

This section explains a four-step process for designing visuals to clarify your presentation structure for a tell/sell presentation as a whole. Think through the four issues in this section first, before you start the detailed process of designing individual charts, described in Section II.

1. Listing your main ideas on an agenda chart

The "agenda" chart—sometimes called the "outline" or "preview" chart—forms the backbone of your presentation. The agenda slide serves as a presentation's "table of contents"; the rest of the visuals in the presentation are like the chapters amplifying the ideas in this table of contents. Therefore, plan your agenda chart carefully and make sure all your subsequent charts follow from, and relate back to, the agenda.

Example: agenda chart

Improve Growth and Efficiency For Bard Company

1. Target specific customer segments.
2. Consolidate operations.
3. Change product mix.

2. Providing evidence on "back-up" charts

The rest of the charts in your presentation are made up of support, or "back-up," visuals. Support each point in your agenda with these back-up slides. Back-up slides may be graphs or diagrams (as described in more detail on pages 116–123) or word charts (as described in more detail on pages 124–127).

Example: graphical "back-up" chart

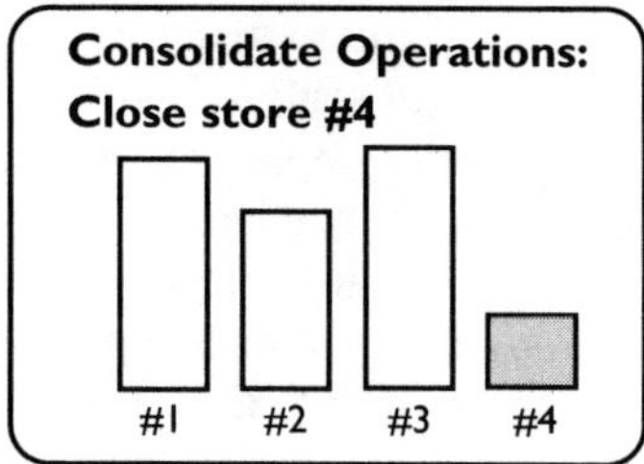

Example: word "back-up" chart

Target Younger Customers

- Pursue couples for engagement and wedding rings.
- Attract high school students for class rings.
- Target parents of teens for gift.

3. Using "message titles" and "stand-alone sense"

Each visual should make sense to someone seeing it for the first time. Put yourself in the shoes of someone who arrived in the middle of your presentation or who missed your presentation and is reading copies of the visuals only. Two methods to increase your audience's ability to understand your visuals are "message titles" and "stand-alone sense."

Using effective message titles Use the headline, usually flush left at the top of each visual, to reinforce the main concept in that visual. If you have a point you are trying to make in your visual, then use a *message title*—a short phrase or sentence with a point to it. Message titles are appropriate for most business presentations because usually you have a conclusion or recommendation to make. If, on the other hand, you do not have a point you are trying to make in your visual, use a *topic title*—that is, a generic phrase or generic term. Topic titles are appropriate only when you don't care what conclusion your audience draws from the data on your visual. Topic titles are easier to write than message titles, in part because they appear automatically on some computer software packages, so be sure to use them only to present uninterpreted data.

Least effective: no title, audience draws conclusion

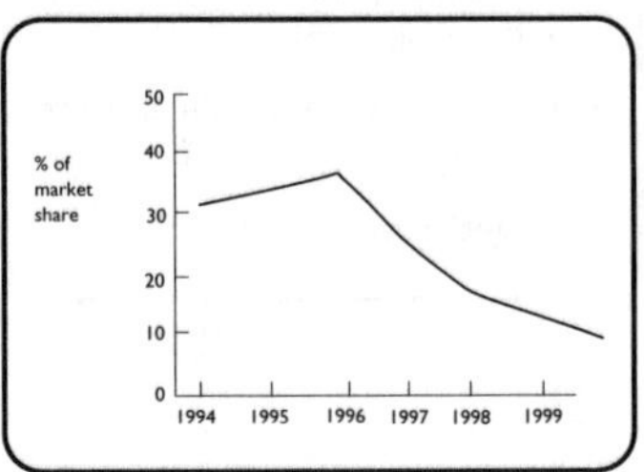

Topic title: audience draws conclusions

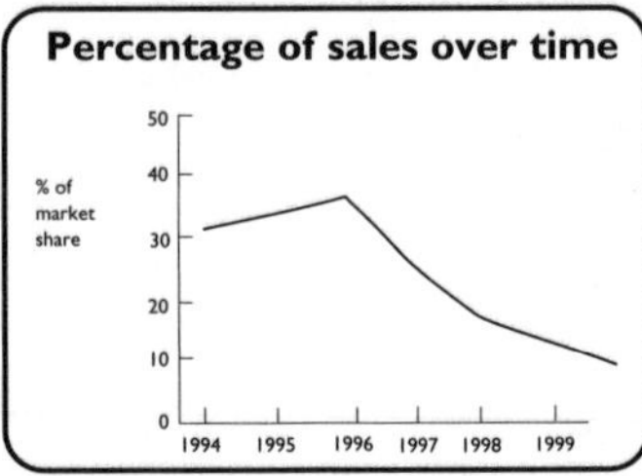

Most effective: message title, speaker draws conclusion

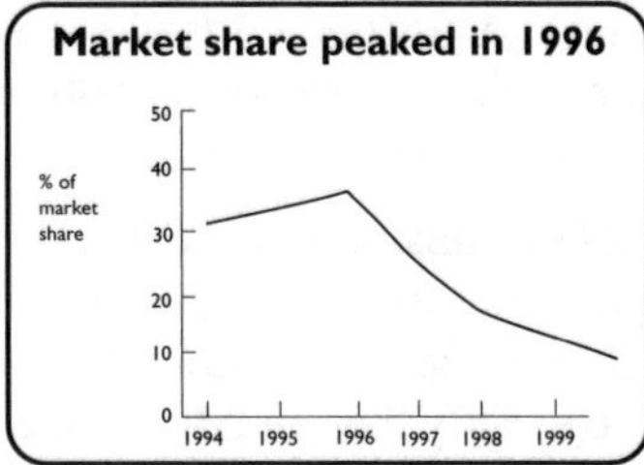

Using "stand-alone sense" Not only should the title make sense on its own, but the wording of the rest of the chart should also make sense to someone seeing it for the first time.

Ineffective: does not make "stand-alone" sense

Hall's Model

High context	**Low context**
• Relationships	• Relationships
• Credibility	• Credibility
• Agreements	• Agreements

Effective: does make "stand-alone" sense

Hall's High-Context and Low-Context Cultures

High-context cultures
- Establish social relationship first.
- Stress personal goodwill credibility.
- Make agreements by general trust.

Low-context cultures
- Get down to business first.
- Stress expertise credibility.
- Make agreements by legalistic contracts.

4. Providing transitions between each visual

Finally, when designing visuals for a tell/sell presentation as a whole, think about how you are going to provide transitions between each visual. Here are three techniques for doing so.

Transition technique #1: Consistency One easy but powerful technique to achieve transitions is to use scrupulous consistency. (1) *Consistency in headings and subheadings:* Each level of headings should adhere to a pattern: use exactly the same font, size, color, and so forth throughout. (2) *Consistency between agenda and "back-ups":* Make sure that the headings in each back-up slide use exactly the same wording as the point in your agenda. For example, if your agenda says "Increase product innovation," the back-up slide should use that exact same wording—not similar wording like "Innovate for new products." (3) *Consistency in numbering system:* If the points are numbered in your agenda, use the same numbering system in your back-up slides.

Transition technique #2: Repeated use of agenda slide Another effective transition tool is to show your agenda slide repeatedly each time you switch to the next main section in your presentation. The following two examples are among the many ways to do so.

Using box to show transition

Improve Growth and Efficiency For Bard Company

1. Target specific customer segments.
2. Consolidate operations.
3. Change product mix.

Using "dim" function to show transition

Improve Growth and Efficiency For Bard Company

1. Target specific customer segments.
2. Consolidate operations.
3. Change product mix.

Transition technique #3: Use of "trackers" If your presentation is especially long or complex, consider using "trackers" on each back-up slide, similar to the "running header" at the top of the pages of this and other book chapters. A "tracker" is a shortened version of the main points on your agenda chart. Here are a few of the many ways to place your trackers.

Tracker: upper left corner

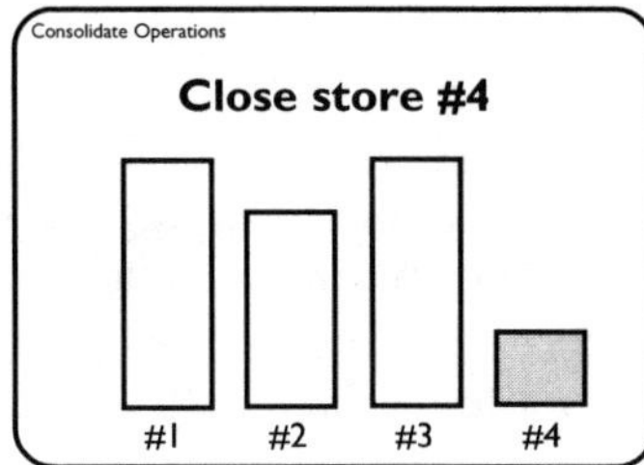

Tracker: lower right corner

Harness the Internet

- Enhance visual presentations.
- Use hyperlinks.
- Institute purchase format.

Design Issues

Tracker: across top of the page

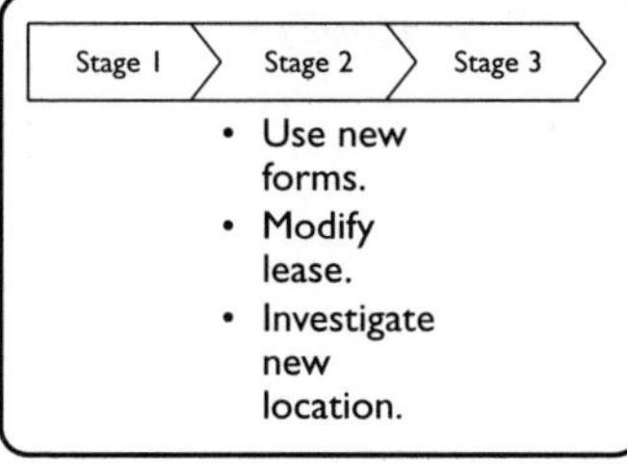

II. DESIGNING EACH INDIVIDUAL CHART

VISUAL AIDS			
I. Designing the presentation as a whole	II. Designing each individual chart	III. Choosing visual aid equipment	IV. Using visual aids effectively

Once you have planned your presentation as a whole, described in the previous section, then design each individual chart. This section covers design techniques to do so: (1) designing graphs to show quantitative data, (2) designing diagrams to show nonquantitative concepts, (3) designing word charts to show main ideas, (4) using typography effectively, (5) using color effectively, and (6) editing each chart.

1. Designing graphs to show quantitative data

Many business presentations include quantitative data, such as financial information, marketing projections, or operations analyses. In many cases, this kind of data will be easier to comprehend and retain if you show it on graphs (such as line charts or bar charts) rather than just in words and figures (such as lists, tabular charts, spreadsheets, or financial statements). For a tell presentation, in which you simply want to present data without any interpretation, you might choose to show quantitative data nongraphically. However, most business presentations are tell/sell style, in which you want to draw conclusions or even recommendations for your audience. In these cases, you will be more effective, emphatic, and persuasive if you use graphs. (See pages 6–7 for more on tell versus sell styles.)

Example: data shown nongraphically
trends not readily apparent

1999		2000	
January	12,543	January	16,985
February	14,371	February	16,106
March	15,998	March	15,422
April	15,004	April	15,010
May	15,281	May	14,564
June	15,742	June	13,820
July	16,101	July	12,489
August	16,254	August	11,376
September	16,378	September	10,897
October	16,495	October	10,178
November	16,397	November	9,657
December	16,463	December	9,281

Example: same data shown graphically
trends more apparent

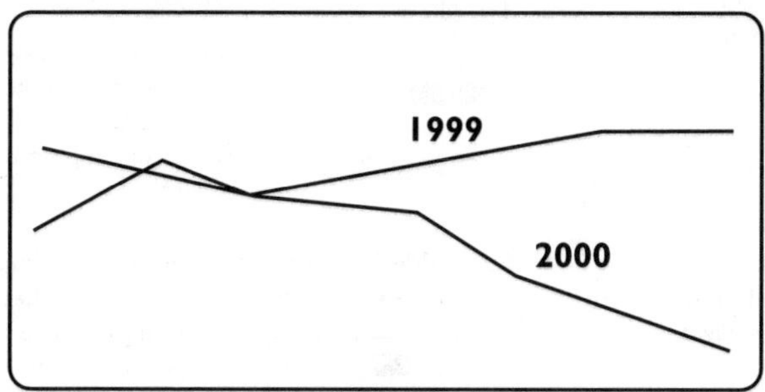

Choose from among the following most prevalent chart types to show quantitative data graphically. In addition to those shown, other chart types include grouped line charts (with more than one line), grouped bar charts (with more than one bar for each item), sliding bar charts (with a line down the middle of the page and bars on the positive and negative sides), and various other combinations.

GRAPHS TO SHOW QUANTITATIVE DATA

If you want to show	Use this graph	Tips
Components of one item → • Percentages • Shares • Proportions	**Pie** 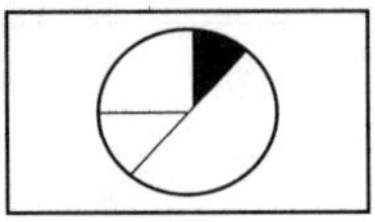 Entire item broken into components	Arrange with most important component at 12 o'clock. If components are equally important, arrange from smallest to largest. Usually, limit to no more than five components.
Rank comparison → • Difference between • Variation • More or less	**Bar** 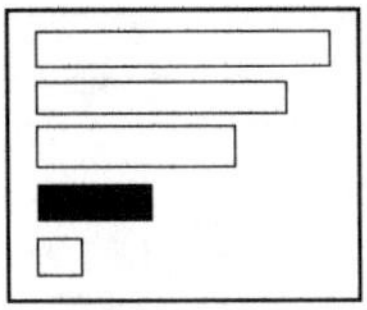	Arrange in order to suit your needs: alphabetical, low to high, high to low. Bar charts run sideways so they are easier to label, and because column charts may imply a time sequence.
Component parts of more than one item → • Percentages • Shares • Proportions	**Subdivided bar or subdivided column** 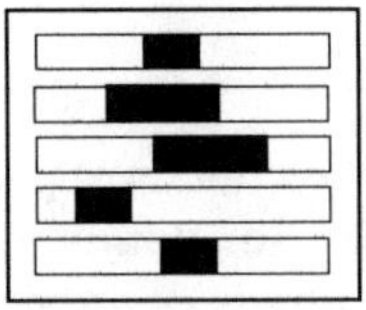 Series of items broken into components	Arrange in order to suit your needs: alphabetical, low to high by a certain component, low to high by item, etc. Bar charts run sideways so they are easier to label, and because column charts may imply a time sequence.

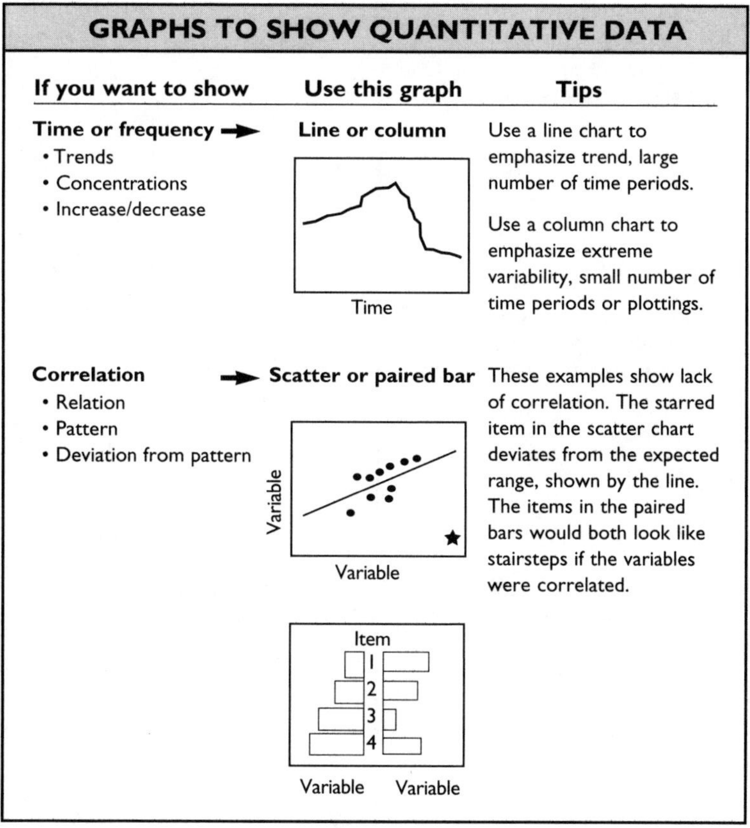

GRAPHS TO SHOW QUANTITATIVE DATA

If you want to show	Use this graph	Tips
Time or frequency → • Trends • Concentrations • Increase/decrease	**Line or column** Time	Use a line chart to emphasize trend, large number of time periods. Use a column chart to emphasize extreme variability, small number of time periods or plottings.
Correlation → • Relation • Pattern • Deviation from pattern	**Scatter or paired bar** Variable Variable Item 1 2 3 4 Variable Variable	These examples show lack of correlation. The starred item in the scatter chart deviates from the expected range, shown by the line. The items in the paired bars would both look like stairsteps if the variables were correlated.

LABELING GRAPHS

1. Preferred option: Label inside section

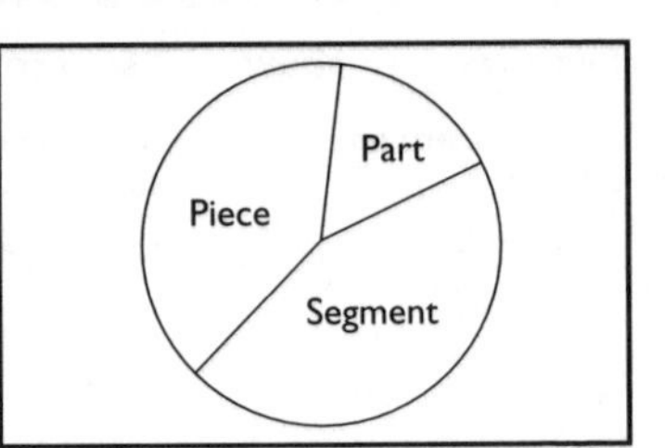

2. Second-best option: Label just outside section

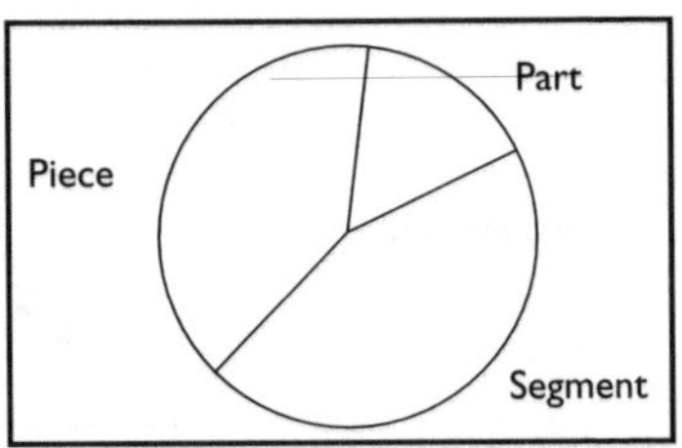

3. Third-best option: Label and connect to section with line

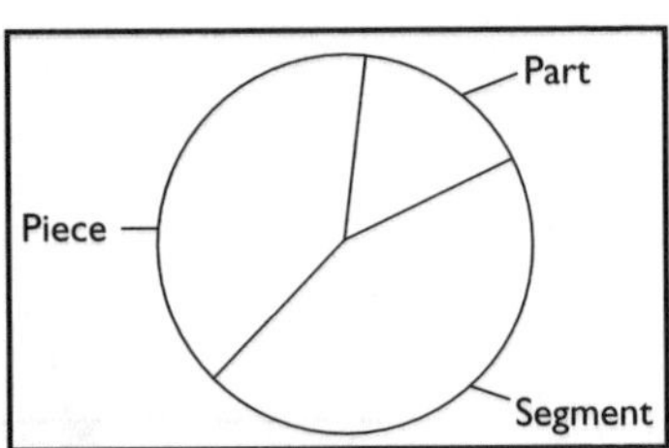

4. Worst option: Use a legend

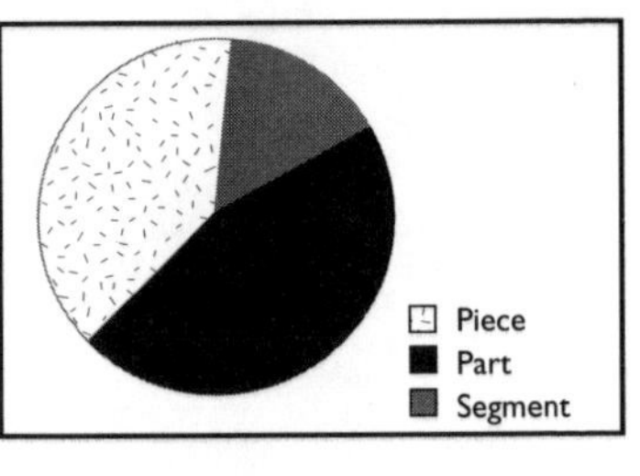

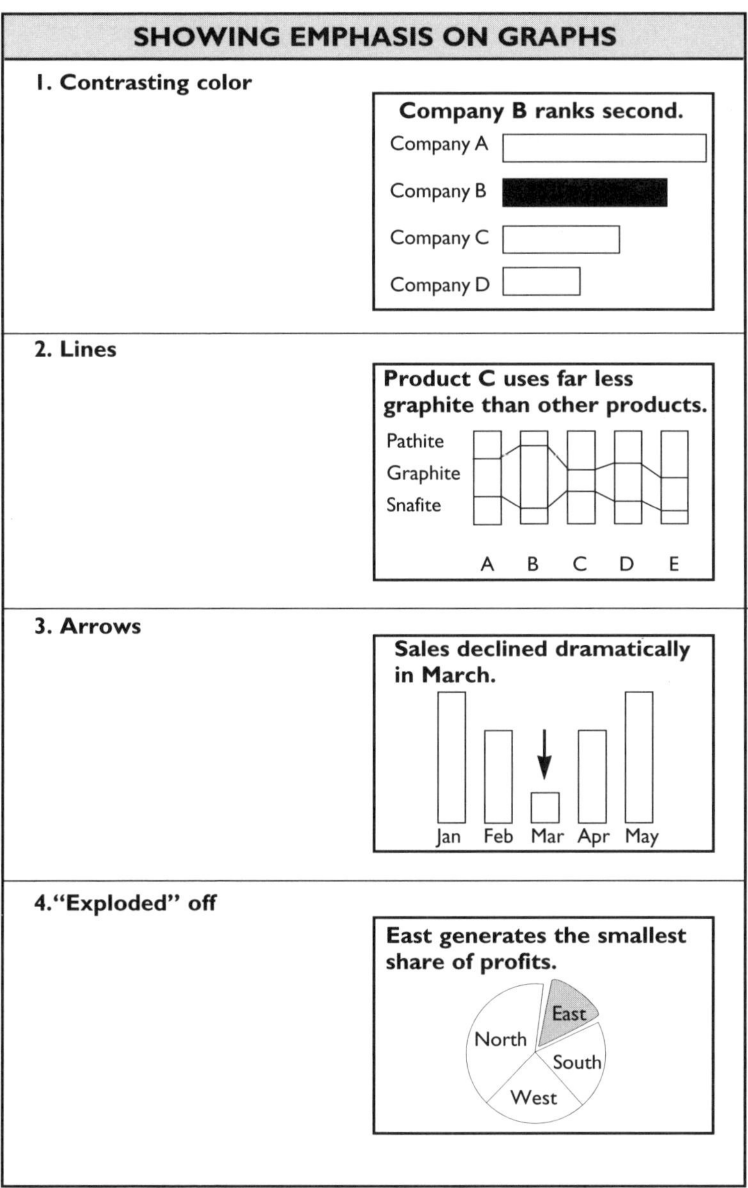
SHOWING EMPHASIS ON GRAPHS
1. Contrasting color
Company B ranks second.
Company A
Company B
Company C
Company D
2. Lines
Product C uses far less graphite than other products.
Pathite
Graphite
Snafite
A B C D E
3. Arrows
Sales declined dramatically in March.
Jan Feb Mar Apr May
4. "Exploded" off
East generates the smallest share of profits.
East
North
South
West

2. Designing diagrams to show nonquantitative concepts

In addition to showing quantitative data visually on graphs, think about ways in which you can show nonquantitative relationships visually on diagrams—especially to add excitement to your visuals and to reach the 40 percent of your audience who are probably visual learners. For example, compare the following two agenda charts:

Agenda example: words only

Improve Growth and Efficiency
For Bard Company

1. Target customer segments.
2. Consolidate operations.
3. Change product mix.

Same agenda: showing relationships visually using a diagram

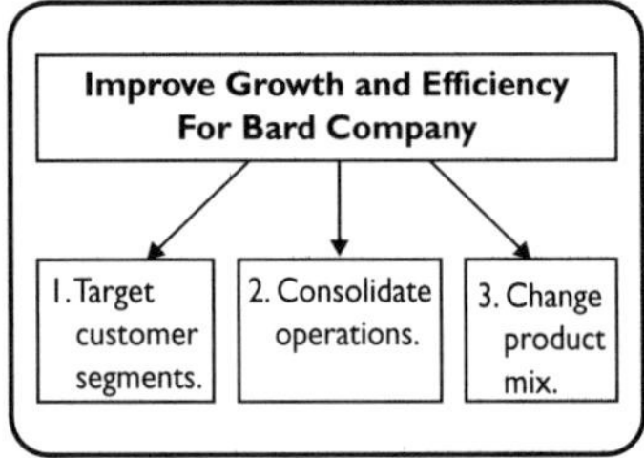

The following examples provide some ideas on how to use diagrams to show nonquantitative data graphically. Other examples of nonquantitative graphs include maps, flowcharts, organization charts, time lines, time-and-activity charts, Gantt charts, and pictograms (e.g., a pound sterling sign representing money). For many more examples of both quantitative and nonquantitative visuals, see Gene Zelazny's book, *Say It With Charts,* listed on page 188.

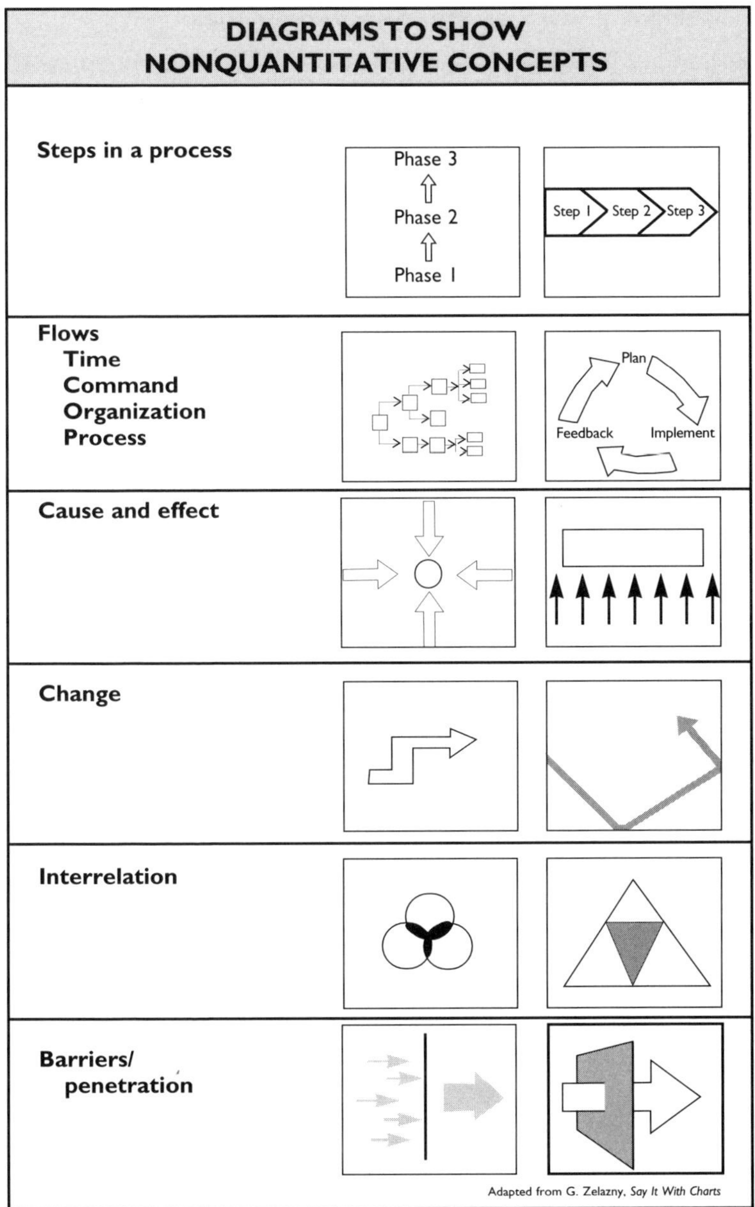

Adapted from G. Zelazny, *Say It With Charts*

3. Designing word charts to show main ideas

Most business presentations include word charts. Word charts are effective for reinforcing the main ideas and structure of your presentation. The most pervasive problem with word charts is that they are overused—in part because it is sometimes easier to include everything than to decide what's really worth including. If you include every point, then you lose your ability to emphasize certain points. This section shows you how to avoid word charts that are unnecessary and wordy, hard to follow because of lack of parallelism, and hard to read because of ineffective indentation. One final word of wisdom: do not undercut your credibility with spelling errors on your word charts. Spelling errors are often more noticeable and glaring on a large screen in front of a group than they are in a document.

Avoid wordiness Avoid overusing word charts, especially boring word-for-word scripts that echo what you are saying throughout the entire presentation. Pare down your word charts to include key words and phrases only.

Ineffective chart: too wordy

INTRODUCTION

Over the past two decades, the waste management industry has undertaken planning as a response to growing markets and an increasingly competitive environment. Understanding historical environmental trends and how they are expected to change is critical to the development of successful strategies of Boford Industries. The purpose of this presentation is to

- Examine the waste management industry today and how it got there
- Assess future trends and their implications
- Discuss how other companies are reacting and changing in response to the external environment

Effective chart: key phrases only

Presentation Agenda
Boford Industries

- Examine historical trends
- Assess future trends
- Analyze competition

Use grammatical parallelism Use grammatical parallelism on word charts—that is, make sure the first word in a series is consistent with the other first words in that series. Like spelling errors, parallelism problems are often more noticeable on visuals than they are on documents because they are projected on a large screen.

Ineffective: not grammatically parallel

Steps to organize internally

1. Establishing formal sales organization
2. Production department responsibilities defined
3. Improve cost-accounting system

Effective: grammatically parallel

Steps to organize internally

1. Establish formal sales organization.
2. Define responsibilities for the production department.
3. Improve cost-accounting system.

Use conceptual parallelism Word charts need to be not only grammatically parallel, but also conceptually parallel—that is, ideas of equal importance should be shown at equal hierarchical levels.

Ineffective: not conceptually parallel
all three lines are not of equal importance

- Change product mix.
- Eliminate product X.
- Concentrate on product Y.

Effective: conceptually parallel
first line is more general;
second and third lines are of equal importance

Change product mix.

- Eliminate product X.
- Concentrate on product Y.

Use effective indentation Finally, word charts are easier to read if entire sections are indented, as shown here.

Ineffective indentation

1. Here is an ineffective example of a numbered section in which the number does not stand out very much because the subsequent lines "wrap around" the number.

1. Here is another ineffective example of a numbered section in which the number does not stand out very much, this time because only the first line is indented.

Effective indentation

1. Here is an example of an effective numbered indentation; all lines in the section are indented equally, so the number "stands out" on its own.

4. Using typography effectively

Typography—including font, size, use of boldface, italics, capitals, and so forth—is an important feature of both graphic and word charts. One of the most prevalent problems with visuals is literally unreadable lettering. Choose your typography with care: large enough, readable, and clear.

Using large enough letters Make sure that each letter is large enough for everyone in your audience to see. The only sure test is to sit in the seat farthest from the visuals and see if you can read the lettering. If you are using computer-generated visuals, normally you should use at least 18-point, and more often 24- or 36-point type.

Readable size

This is 24-point type.

Less readable size

This is 12-point type. It is fine for written documents, but too small for visual aids.

Using standard capitalization Except for very short titles, capitalize only the first letter of a sentence or phrase.

Readable capitalization

This is standard capitalization. Only the first letter of the phrase or sentence is capitalized.

Less readable capitalization

This Is Not Standard Capitalization. Capitalizing Every Word Slows Down Your Readers.

Least readable capitalization

THIS IS ALL CAPITALS. THE LACK OF SIZE VARIATION WITH ALL CAPITAL LETTERS MAKES THIS KIND OF TEXT THE HARDEST TO READ.

Choosing a readable font As explained on pages 55–56, serif fonts are the easiest to read. *Serif fonts*, such as Times, are those with extenders on the ends of most letters; *sans serif fonts*, such as Helvetica, do not have extenders on the ends of letters. A sans serif font with all capital letters is the hardest to read, as shown in the following example.

Ineffective typography: sans serif, all capitals

THIS IS SANS SERIF FONT, SET IN ALL CAPITAL LETTERS. THE LACK OF SIZE VARIATION WITH ALL CAPITALS AND NO SERIFS MAKES THIS COMBINATION THE HARDEST TO READ.

Avoiding letterjunk Letterjunk is the gratuitous use of lettering that calls undue attention to itself or is simply hard to read. Examples of letterjunk include too many typographical elements (such as boldface plus italics plus underlining plus all capitals all at once), outline and shadow styles, arty fonts, and jarring font variations.

Ineffective typography: examples of letterjunk

THIS SHOWS BOLDFACE + UNDERLINING + ALL CAPS!

This shows shadow style.

This shows an "arty" font.

This **shows** *jarring* font VARIATIONS.

5. Using color effectively

One of the biggest advantages of computer software programs is the easy availability of colors they provide. Use of color can make your visuals look attractive, lively, professional, and easily remembered; prioritize important ideas; and show your structure. On the other hand, for some audiences, use of color can come across as too slick, too expensive-looking, and counter to cultural norms or expectations. If using color is appropriate, here are some suggestions for doing so.

Use color to reinforce your structure Viewers sense color relationships clearly and quickly, so they will stay better attuned to your structure if you use color in a consistent pattern. Throughout the entire presentation, use exactly the same pattern (including not only color, but also size and font) for your main headings, secondary headings, trackers, and so forth. Unfortunately, virtually all of the standardized templates available on computer software packages are inappropriate for most business presentations because they tend to be fanciful, cutesy, and draw too much attention to themselves. Therefore, design your own color template—a combination of background and foreground colors—to use consistently throughout the presentation for a unified look. If possible, select your colors using the screen on which you will be presenting, not your computer monitor; colors will vary significantly on screen.

- *Background color:* Select your background color based on the equipment you will be using: for a well-lit room (e.g., most overhead projectors), choose a light background, such as pale blue or white; for a darkened room (e.g., most multimedia projectors), choose a dark background, such as dark blue or black.
- *Foreground color:* Your foreground color—that is, for titles and text—should contrast sharply with the background color (e.g., bright yellow on bright blue, but not light blue on dark blue).

Use color to emphasize important ideas. Viewers will look at anything that is not black and white first, so another effective use of color is for emphasis or to show priority.

- *Tie the colored element to your message title.* For example, if your message title is about a certain "slice of the pie" on a pie chart, use a bright, contrasting color for that slice only. Beware of computer software programs that automatically color every piece of the pie in a different color: this will overwhelm your audience with too much visual stimulation.

- *Do not use color for unemphatic elements.* Do not use color for unemphatic elements such as the bullet points themselves or a line under the title.

Do not overuse color. Do not weaken the power of color by overusing it. Do not use color just because it is available; use it only if it enhances your message. Do not just color to decorate; use it to communicate. Always combine visual appeal with meaning. Often, you must override default use of color in computer software, such as every column or every line in a different color.

Design expert Jan White refers to the overuse of color as the "fruit salad effect." White recommends using two colors in addition to black, because "the more colors there are, the more difficult it is to remember the meaning each carries. Keep the code simple." He sees four distinct colors as the maximum. For much more information on use of color, see his book, *Color for Impact*, listed on page 188.

Choose colors carefully In addition to the preceding design considerations for color, keep in mind cultural and physical issues.

- *Cultural connotations of color:* In the Anglo-American culture, the cool colors connote calmness and authority; the warm colors connote dynamism and activity; the dark colors (black, gray, dark gray) evoke power and strength. Use of red with monetary totals can imply "in the red." However, these emotional overtones vary by individual and by culture. For example, although black connotes death in Western cultures, the death color is white in many Eastern cultures, yellow in many Moslem cultures, and purple in many Latin American cultures. As other examples, the colors of a country's flag will have a special meaning in that country, the colors of an organization's corporate identity will have special meaning for that organization.
- *Color-blindness:* Remember that 8 percent of men and 1 percent of women are color-blind, so avoid using green and red as contrasting colors. Blue is a universally recognized color.

6. Editing each chart

Just as you would microedit your writing, you also microedit your visuals. In addition to cutting wordiness, edit overload and extraneous graphics.

Avoid overload Avoid overloaded text or graphic visuals that include too much complexity for one chart. Audience members may end up reading and pondering these charts instead of listening to you; at worst, they may get completely lost. Therefore, for each visual, decide what is more important for the audience to see. If you find yourself with an overloaded visual, such as the one shown in the figures that follow, you might choose to either (1) simplify it so that the key ideas, figures, or trends are emphasized, as illustrated in the bottom of the figure, or (2) cut it so that one section is shown in detail, or (3) break it into a series of overlays or progressive "builds," each of which shows an added layer of detail.

Ineffective chart: overloaded

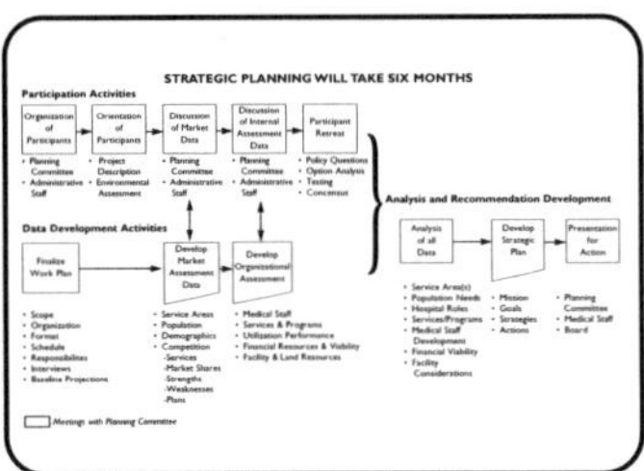

Effective chart: simplified to show key trends only

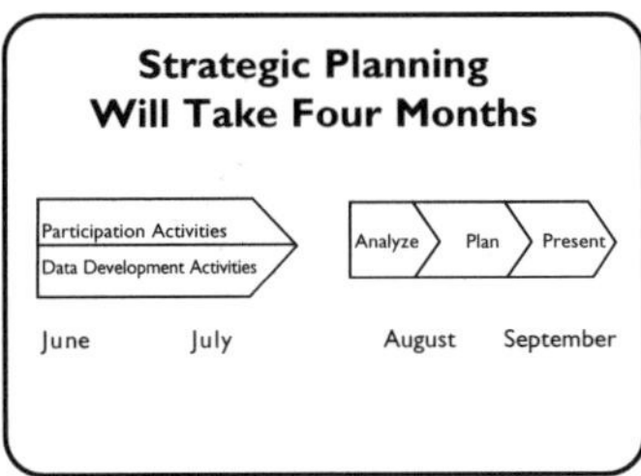

Delete chartjunk To use the term coined by visual aids expert Edward Tufte, delete *chartjunk*—any extraneous design elements that do not contribute to your message, including the following:

- *Decorations* that do not add informational value—such as unnecessary shading, unnecessary borders, misleading three-dimensional effects, unnecessary decorations, and "op art" crosshatching.
- *Legends* and confusing cross-coding systems that take longer for your audience to comprehend than labeling the parts of the pie charts, bar charts, line charts, and so forth right on the pie, bar, or lines themselves.

Ineffective chart: chartjunk

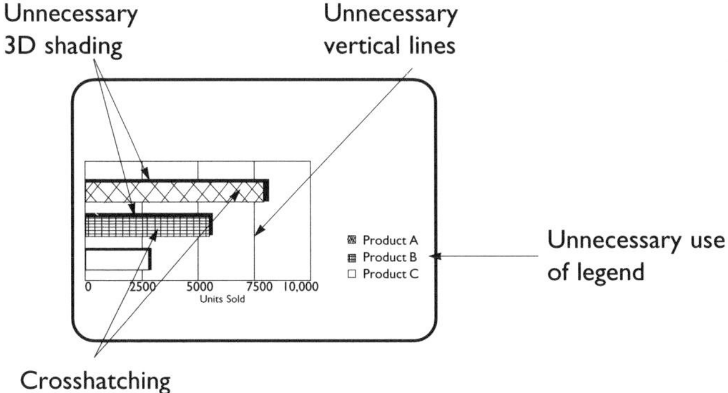

Effective chart: no chartjunk

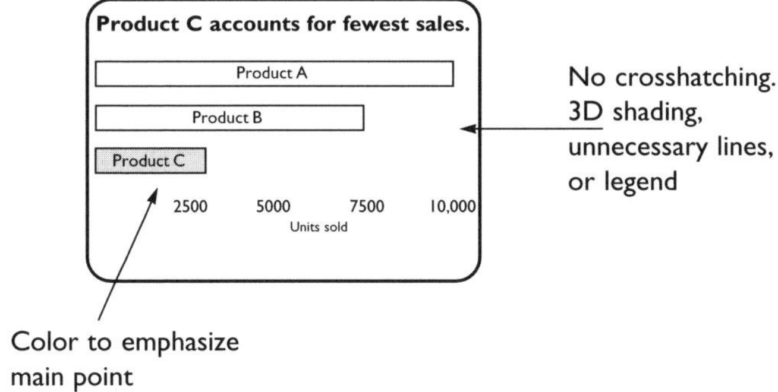

III. CHOOSING VISUAL AID EQUIPMENT

VISUAL AIDS			
I. Designing the presentation as a whole	II. Designing each individual chart	III. Choosing visual aid equipment	IV. Using visual aids effectively

To choose your visual aid equipment, first consider three sets of issues: (1) Find out if your audience, organization, or culture expects you to use a certain kind of equipment. (2) Consider the size of your audience; for example, a flipchart might work well for a group of 10; it would be unreadable for a group of 80. (3) Finally, be realistic about the equipment and resources you have available.

Only after you have answered these three questions, think about the characteristics intrinsic in the various kinds of equipment—which are described next, with their advantages and disadvantages listed on the chart on pages 134–135.

Multimedia projection systems Multimedia systems project images and sounds from a personal computer, the web, videotape, audiotape, or clip media banks. Multimedia projectors may be either portable or nonportable.

- *Nonportable:* (1) CRT (cathode ray tube) projectors offer the best resolution for full-screen multimedia projection, but they are not as bright as their LCD (liquid crystal display) counterparts. (2) Self-illuminating plasma technology offers good resolution and space-saving installation.
- *Portable:* (1) LCD projectors (with a self-contained light source) offer excellent resolution and are brighter than CRT projectors. Some models employ DLP (digital light processing) technology. (2) LCD projection panels (using an overhead projector as a light source) are lower quality and are falling out of use. (3) Group data-display television monitors (ranging from 30 to 40 inches diagonally) offer the best resolution, are the best for showing extended spreadsheets or text, and are more versatile than regular television monitors for teleconferencing; however, they can only be used with small to medium-sized groups, and are not easily portable. (4) Regular computer screens (ranging from 14 to 21 inches diagonally) may be used with small groups only.

Still projection systems Three varieties of still projectors include overhead projectors, 35-mm slide projectors, and CCD digital cameras.

- *Overhead projectors* are extremely versatile: you can write on them real time, you can prepare them entirely in advance, and you can refer back to a slide or change the order.
- *35-mm slide projectors* have the highest resolution and truest color of all the still projection systems. However, you have to fast-forward to get to the slide you want to show.
- *CCD digital cameras*—also known as document cameras or copy stands—create a digital image and magnify it onto a screen. These are often used to magnify and digitize documents or objects during a videoconference.

Animated projection systems Video and film appeal to entertainment sensibilities, but required a darkened room.

Boards and charts These are good for group discussions.

- *Traditional black or white boards* may encourage group discussion because they are low-tech and unintimidating but do not provide hard copy.
- *Electronic copy boards* provide hard copy of something you place on or write on the board. In teleconferencing, they can be annotated real time in one location.
- *"Live" boards* can be written on from computers, real time from multiple locations.
- *Flipcharts* may be prepared in advance or written as you speak. Pages may be attached to the walls for further discussion, with tape, tacks, static-cling, or adhesive sticky notes.

Hard copy Since one of the disadvantages of oral presentations is their lack of hard copy for the audience to keep, presenters often use some form of handouts. See pages 137–138 for tips on how to use them.

- *Presentation "decks" or "discussion packets"* are hard copies of all the presentation slides, usually distributed at the beginning of the presentation, sometimes in advance.
- *Handouts* are given during the presentation—usually detailed handouts at the exact time when you are discussing a certain issue or summary handouts at the end of the presentation.
- *Presentation "leave-behinds"* are identical to decks, a packet containing a hard copy of all the slides, but are distributed at the end. Electronic handouts are distributed on the network or disk.

VISUAL AID EQUIPMENT		
Equipment	**Main advantages**	**Main disadvantages**
	For all multimedia projections	
Multimedia projection systems	Can use input from the web, PCs, video, etc.; can use animation (e.g., show "swoop," etc.); can use a variety of "build" techniques; can plug into audience's networked computers; can input numbers real time	May be complicated to use; usually need darkened room; not good for facilitating group discussion; cannot annotate real time; may appear too slick for some audiences
	All of the above plus	***All of the above plus***
Nonportable	CRT best resolution for full screen; plasma saves installation space; both good for large groups	Not portable
Portable	LCD excellent resolution	Not easily portable
	TV	TV display can be seen by medium-sized groups only
	Computer	Computer screen can be seen by small groups only
	For all still projection systems	
Still projection systems	Portable; less technically complex than multimedia; compatibility problems unlikely; easy to use	No animation; cannot use "build" techniques
	All of the above plus	***All of the above plus***
Overhead projectors	Versatile: can write on them real time or prepare completely in advance; "random access": easy to refer back to a previous slide; can make image large or small	Somewhat darkened room; projector may block audience view; may be awkward to manipulate; may appear old-fashioned to some audiences
35-mm slide projectors	Highest resolution and truest color of all projection systems; projection does not block audience view visible to large audiences (e.g., in an auditorium)	Darkened room; may be time consuming to produce 35-mm slides; "serial access": hard to refer back to a previous slide easily; cannot annotate real time
CCD digital cameras	Projects image from any hard copy of 3D object	Less effective resolution than overheads or slides

Equipment	Main advantages	Main disadvantages
	For all animated projection systems	
Animated projection systems	Animated; visible to large audiences (e.g., in an auditorium)	Darkened room; "serial access": hard to refer back to specific section
	All of the above plus	***All of the above plus***
Video projections	Interruptions possible using start, stop, rewind, pause; audiences with networked PCs can access video directly	Format must be compatible in different locations, especially in different countries (PALS vs. VHS)
	For all boards and charts	
Boards and charts	Brightly lit room; good for facilitating group discussion; can annotate real time	Inability to show complex images; usually too small to be seen by a large group
	All of the above plus	***All of the above plus***
Traditional black or white boards	May encourage discussion because low tech, unintimidating	Must erase to regain free space; no hard copy; may appear unprofessional to some audiences
Electronic copy boards	Provides digitalized hard copy of document computer files or 2D object; can be annotated in real time in one location; can be viewed on computer screen in multiple locations	Must erase to regain free space; same limitations as a scanner, free format
"Live" boards	All of the above, plus (1) can be annotated on-line in multiple locations; (2) may have application-sharing capability	
Flipcharts	No electronics problems; may be attached to walls for further discussion	Large and clumsy to transport
	For all handouts	
	Provides hard copy; shows complex data; can be used for audience note taking	Audience can read ahead and become distracted from what you are saying

IV. USING VISUAL AIDS EFFECTIVELY

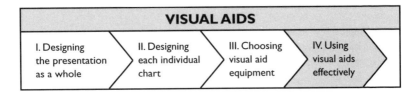

VISUAL AIDS			
I. Designing the presentation as a whole	II. Designing each individual chart	III. Choosing visual aid equipment	IV. Using visual aids effectively

All your work composing and designing prepared visual aids will be wasted unless you use them effectively during the presentation itself. This section covers techniques for using visuals effectively by (1) using visuals prepared in advance (in tell/sell presentations) and (2) facilitating group discussions with visuals (in consult/join situations).

1. Using prepared tell/sell visuals

Here are seven suggestions for using tell/sell visuals gracefully, unobtrusively, and effectively.

Become familiar with your equipment. Get extremely comfortable with your equipment to avoid undercutting your credibility and confidence if you use it wrong. Practice with your equipment physically: actually turn it on, press the buttons, use the mouse or remote control, flip the pages, insert the cassette, position the slides, write large enough, and so forth. Practice with any given piece of equipment long enough that you can use it casually, without thinking.

Show only the chart you are discussing. Make sure your audience will see only the same information you are discussing at a given moment.

- *Opening:* For your presentation opening, figure out a way to cover any visuals you don't want people to see yet. For example, use a "title page," a blank screen or page, or leave the projector turned off until you get to your first chart.
- *After each visual:* When you are no longer discussing a visual, get it out of sight. For example, insert a blank slide if you aren't using another visual for several minutes; erase the board; or turn to a blank flipchart page.

Introduce each visual. Before you show a visual, state your transition out loud, for example, "So how did we perform last year?" or "Now Vipal will discuss our performance last year." Then show the slide with an introductory remark, such as "You can see we performed best in the third quarter." Let the audience digest the slide for a moment. For a simple text visual, you might say "As this agenda chart shows, I will cover three main topics today" (then list and point to each of the three). For a complicated graphic visual, explain the graph in general first; you might say, "As you can see, this graph covers each month of the last fiscal year on the horizontal axis (point to it) and sales in thousands of dollars on the vertical axis (point to it). In particular, I'd like to draw your attention to the May figures (point to it)."

Use "build" effectively. Another big advantage of computer software programs is their "build" function. For particularly complex charts, introduce them section by section, instead of showing them in their entirety all at once (e.g., build the axis first, then add and explain each line). Even for simple word charts—since your audience will always read whatever is in front of them regardless of what you are saying—use "build" to add new lines of information. For most business audiences, choose "standard dim" to dim your previous points; for particularly young or high-tech audiences only, use special effects such as "flying build" or "dissolve build." With overhead projectors, you can build by using a series of overlays or a cardboard mask to systematically uncover each point.

Use handouts effectively. Assume people will read whatever is in front of them; they can read faster than you can speak. Therefore, if possible, control when to distribute handouts.

- *At the beginning:* At the beginning, distribute (1) general handouts, such as the agenda, (2) handouts with blank space for audience note taking, and (3) presentation "decks" or "discussion packets."

- *Not until you discuss:* Distribute handouts on detailed information that is too complex for a chart only at that specific point in your presentation when you are discussing it. Remember to give the audience some time to read what they were just handed.
- *At the end:* Save detailed summary handouts you don't want your audience to read ahead, presentation "leave-behinds," and handouts downloaded from the screen, to distribute at the end of the presentation.

Use pointing effectively. Pointing is an extremely effective technique. It enhances your nonverbal delivery by giving you something to do with your hand, and it enhances your audience comprehension by what you're saying with what they're seeing. Here are some tips for effective pointing.

- *Point to the exact place.* Point at the exact place on your chart you want your audience to look; do not merely gesture vaguely in the direction of your visuals.
- *Face your audience.* Regardless of whether you are right- or left-handed, always point with whichever hand is closer to the screen or chart, so you will not put your back to the audience.
- *Point on the screen itself.* If possible, step back and point on the screen itself, not on the overhead projector; projectors magnify any nervousness you might be showing in your hands or fingers.
- *Point with your hand.* If possible, point with your hand—not with any kind of pointer—unless you absolutely cannot reach what you are pointing to otherwise. Pointers usually cause fidgeting and shaking problems; if you must use a pointer, practice with it extensively to avoid these problems.

Look at your audience. Many speakers get so engrossed with their equipment or charts that they forget to look at the audience. Remember you are there to interact with your audience, not with your visuals. Practice maintaining your eye contact while using visuals.

- *Using projectors:* If you are using any kind of projector, face your audience—not the screen, the projector, or the computer. If possible, stand back next to the screen. If you stand next to the projector or the computer itself, you may block some people's view of the screen.
- *Writing:* If you are writing as you speak, avoid writing for long periods of time. Write key phrases only; use abbreviation. You also might trace over figures you have drawn very faintly in advance to avoid having your back to the audience for too long.

2. Using consult/join visuals

On pages 95–103, we discussed consult/join meetings in which you enhance audience interaction. In these situations, use visual aids to record participant comments, to summarize action plans, and to form the basis for meeting minutes. The following section explains how to use visuals to facilitate group discussions.

Why use visuals to facilitate discussion In a consult/join meeting, you should virtually always record ideas on some kind of visual, such as a board or chart. Why?

- *For accuracy:* Recording ideas publicly ensures accuracy and a record of what was said.
- *For morale:* Recording ideas publicly also makes people feel heard and appreciated, even if their ideas are rejected later.
- *For timing control:* Besides making everyone feel included and heard, writing on visuals may be used to control timing. If people talk too long or repetitively, recording their points may assure them of feeling heard, so you can move on.
- *For a permanent record:* From your charts, you can come up with a permanent record at the end of the meeting, either electronically if you have an electronic board or by writing minutes from the charts.

How to plan logistics for visuals Although most of the work involved with recording a discussion goes on during the session itself, be sure to plan your charts and logistics in advance.

- *Tie them to the agenda.* Use the same wording and organization on both your visuals and your agenda.
- *Decide on headings.* Your headings in consult/join visuals are just as important as they are in tell/sell visuals. Since you want your audience to offer ideas, each heading should keep them reminded of what they are discussing. Therefore, decide in advance what your main headings are going to be. In most cases, write the main headings up in advance, leaving space to fill in as ideas are generated; for example, list various options across the board or provide a heading describing what you are brainstorming about at the top of a chart.

- *Think about a visual framework.* Is there any visual framework you might use to enhance the group discussion? For example, use a T-chart to discuss opposites or contrasts, a three-column chart or matrix to organize information, a Venn diagram to show overlapping issues, or a Gantt chart to discuss a time frame. (See the Howell book in the bibliography, page 187, for much more on visual frameworks.)
- *Consider room arrangements.* Think about the logistics of the room—such as where to put empty charts and where to post filled-in charts.

How to choose equipment Think about your equipment choice in advance. Regardless of what equipment you choose, make sure it works; especially, check to make sure all the markers work.

- *Flipcharts:* One popular equipment choice for group discussions is flipcharts. Flipcharts can be attached to the walls by tape or self-stick adhesive paper, and you can take them with you for a permanent record of the session.
- *Electronic boards:* Electronic "copy boards" provide a hard copy of what was written on them. Electronic "live boards," used in teleconferencing, can provide hard copy and be annotated in multiple locations.
- *Overheads:* Finally, although it is technically possible to use overheads to record people's ideas, remember that some people associate overheads with a tell/sell presentation, rather than with a discussion, and may be less likely to talk.

Why consider using a scribe Instead of writing on the visuals yourself, consider asking someone else to serve as scribe. However, determining what is recorded and when is a tool of control and influence, so if you use someone else as scribe, make it extremely clear in advance how you will work together: you may, for example, want to specify that the scribe records only the specific wording you signal to him or her to write down during the session; or you may empower the scribe to record at his or her discretion. Using a scribe offers three benefits.

- *Enhances facilitation:* Managing the discussion will be much easier for you, because you don't have to talk and write at the same time.
- *Improves legibility:* The scribe can write more carefully and you can select someone with neat handwriting.
- *Saves time:* Perhaps most importantly, using a scribe saves time, because you can go on to discuss the next point while the scribe is still recording the previous point.

How to record on visuals Writing to record participants' ideas is not easy. Here are six suggestions to improve your effectiveness.

- *Record accurately.* If you are facilitating the meeting, paraphrase the comment verbally, or ask the speaker to summarize his or her own point before recording it. If you are not facilitating, but just serving as scribe, either record the facilitator's paraphrase, or, if the facilitator has not paraphrased verbally, check with the speaker, verbally (e.g., "OK?" or "Is this what you mean?") or nonverbally (e.g., questioning eye contact), to make sure what you've written is accurate.
- *Record essential phrases only.* Make sure you record essential words and phrases only. Avoid boring your audience and wasting time by laboriously writing long complex sentences.
- *Include all comments.* Write down everybody's comments—not just some people's. You don't want to appear to be ignoring people or leaving people out. Recording their ideas on your visuals does not necessarily mean you agree with them; instead, it means you hear and acknowledge them. In fact, you may very well end up recording contradictory ideas. That is perfectly appropriate in an interactive session; you can go back later and evaluate the comments.
- *Keep charts in full view.* Be sure to write and post all charts in full view of the group throughout the meeting, so everyone can see what's going on.
- *Use large enough lettering.* Make sure your writing is large enough. Before the session, seat yourself in the last row to check your lettering size. You may be surprised how large you need to write.
- *Write neatly.* You can learn to write more neatly as a result of practice—or, if you simply have messy writing, consider using a scribe to record for you.

See the checklists on pages 160–161 for a summary of all the speaking issues covered in Chapters V, VI, and VII: structure, visual aids, and nonverbal delivery.

CHAPTER VII OUTLINE

I. Tell/sell nonverbal skills
   1. Body language
   2. Vocal qualities
   3. Space and objects
   4. Practice and arrangements
   5. Physical relaxation
   6. Mental relaxation
   7. Last-minute relaxation

II. Consult/join nonverbal skills
   1. Attending skills
   2. Encouraging skills
   3. Following skills

CHAPTER VII

Speaking: Nonverbal Skills

Your words (Chapter V) and your visual aids (Chapter VI) make up only a portion of what you communicate. In fact, experts estimate that 65 to 90 percent of what you communicate is nonverbal. This chapter covers those nonverbal messages you send—the way you appear and sound to others.

The first part of the chapter covers nonverbal delivery skills to use in tell/sell presentations. The second part concentrates on the nonverbal listening skills to use in various consult/join situations. The examples in this chapter are based on Anglo-American business practices; keep in mind that nonverbal communication varies widely across different cultures, as discussed on pages 29–31.

NONVERBAL SKILLS		
Section in this chapter:	**I. Tell/Sell Nonverbal Skills**	**II. Consult/Join Nonverbal Skills**
Who speaks most:	You	Your audience
Purposes:	To inform or To persuade	To understand
Typical situations:	Tell/sell presentations	Questions and answers Consult/join meetings One-to-one conversations

I. TELL/SELL NONVERBAL SKILLS

NONVERBAL SKILLS		
Section in this chapter:	**I. Tell/Sell Nonverbal Skills**	**II. Consult/Join Nonverbal Skills**
Who speaks most:	You	Your audience
Purposes:	To inform or To persuade	To understand
Typical situations:	Tell/sell presentations	Questions and answers Consult/join meetings One-to-one conversations

Nonverbal delivery skills include body language, vocal qualities, and space and objects around you.

1. Body language

Keep in mind these five elements of body language.

Posture Effective speakers exhibit poise through their posture.

- Stand in a relaxed, professional manner—comfortably upright, squarely facing your audience, with your weight balanced and distributed evenly. Your feet should be aligned under your shoulders—neither too close nor too far apart.
- Watch out for rocking or swaying side to side, back and forth, or up and down on your toes. Beware also of slouching or keeping your weight on one side or on the podium. Finally, avoid "frozen" poses, such as the stiff "Attention!" stance.

Body movement Body movement varies by personality and room size.

- Move naturally. You don't have to stand stock still or plan every move. Examples of effective body movement include leaning forward to emphasize a point or walking back to point to your visual aid.
- Avoid random, nervous, quick, or constant movements.

Hand and arm gestures Effective speakers use their hands the same way they would conversationally; also they use them to integrate their visual aids, as explained on pages 136–138.

- Let your hands do whatever they would be doing if you were speaking to one person instead of to a group. Be yourself: some people use expansive gestures; others are more reserved. For example, use them to move conversationally, to be still for a while, to emphasize a point, to describe an object, or to point to a particular line on your visual aid.
- Avoid putting your hands in any one position and leaving them there without change—such as the "figleaf" (hands clasped in front), the "parade rest" (hands clasped in back), the "gunshot wound" (hand clutching opposite arm), or the "podium clutch." Avoid nervous-looking gestures, such as ear–tugging or arm–scratching. Finally, avoid "authority killers" like flipping your hair or waving your arms randomly.

Facial expression Your facial expression should also look natural as it would in conversation.

- Keep your face relaxed to look interested and animated. Vary your expression according to the subject and the occasion.
- Avoid a stony, deadpan expression; also, avoid inappropriate facial expression, such as smiling when you are talking about something sad or negative.

Eye contact Eye contact is a crucial nonverbal skill. It makes possible what communication expert Lynn Russell calls the "listening/speaking connection": with good eye contact, (1) the audience feels connected with you and (2) you can read the audience's reactions.

- Look throughout the entire room, establishing momentary (that is, about two-second) contact with individuals in your audience. You might try, for starters, looking at the friendly faces; their nodding and smiling will encourage you. Eventually, however, you should look at everyone—especially the key decision makers in the group. You don't need to keep 100 percent eye contact; you may need to look away briefly to think. If, after your presentation, you can remember what the people in your audience looked like, you had good eye contact.
- Avoid looking constantly at a manuscript or notecards, at the visual aids or screen, at the middle of the back of the room, at the ceiling, or at the floor. Don't show a preference for looking at one side of the room or the other. Finally, avoid fake eye contact—such as "eye dart," eyes moving back and forth very rapidly, or the back-and-forth "lighthouse scan."

2. Vocal qualities

Many people underestimate the importance of the voice in establishing credibility. See page 151 for vocal relaxation exercises.

Inflection and volume The term *inflection* refers to variation in your pitch that creates an expressive, nonmonotonous sound; *volume* refers to how loudly you speak.

- Speak with expressiveness and enthusiasm, in a warm, pleasant tone, with pitch variety. Use volume appropriate for the size of the room. Breathe deeply and fully.
- Avoid the common problem of speaking in a dull, robotic monotone that sounds as if you are bored. Do not speak too quietly to be heard or too loudly for the size of the room. Watch out for two particular volume problems: volume drops at the ends of your sentences and volume drops when you use visual aids.

Rate Rate is the speed at which you speak.

- Vary your rate somewhat to avoid droning. Generally, keep it slow enough to be understood but fast enough to maintain energy. Use pauses, or "mental punctuation," before or after a key term, to separate items in a series, or to indicate a major break in thought.
- Watch out for speaking at a monotonous, constant rate. An ineffective rate lacks pauses or variation: if too slow, it may bore your audience; if too fast, it may lose them.

Fillers Fillers are verbal pauses—like *uh*, *er*, *um*, and *ya know*.

- Pause during your presentation to collect your thoughts. You don't need to fill the pause with a filler.
- Don't overreact if you notice a few fillers; everybody uses them occasionally. If you diagnose a distracting, habitual, overuse of fillers, try asking a colleague to signal you every time you use one.

Enunciation Enunciation is the clarity of your articulation.

- Pronounce your words clearly, without mumbling, running words together, leaving out syllables, or dropping final consonants.
- Avoid mumbling, which may be perceived as sounding uneducated or hurried. Avoid running words together—as in *gonna* or *wanna*—which is often associated with talking too fast. Avoid leaving out syllables, as in *guvmint*. Finally, avoid dropping final consonants, as in *thousan'*, *jus'*, or *goin'*.

3. Space and objects

Another component of nonverbal communication is the use of space and objects around you. Objects and space affect four sets of choices: seating arrangements, speaker height and distance, use of objects, and dress.

Seating The way you arrange the chairs for a presentation will communicate nonverbally what kind of interaction you want to have with your audience. Choose straight lines of chairs for the least interactive sessions. Choose horseshoe–shaped or u-shaped lines of chairs to encourage more interaction. For smaller groups choose either (1) a rectangular table, with a person seated at the head, to emphasize the power of the leader or (2) a round table to encourage equality among participants.

Height and distance The higher you are in relationship to your audience, the more formal the atmosphere you are establishing nonverbally. Therefore, the most formal presentations might be delivered from a stage or a platform. In a semiformal situation, you stand while your audience sits. To make the situation even less formal, place yourself and your audience at the same level: sit together around a table or seat yourself in front of the group. Similarly, the closer you are, the less formal you appear.

Objects The more objects you place between yourself and the audience, the more formal the interaction. To increase formality, use a podium, desk, or table between yourself and the audience. To decrease formality, stand or sit without any articles of furniture between you and your audience.

Dress What you wear also communicates something to your audience. Dress to project the image that you want to create. Dress appropriately for the audience, the occasion, the organization, and the culture. For instance, what is appropriate in the fashion industry may be totally inappropriate in the banking industry. Finally, don't wear clothes that will distract from what you are saying—such as exaggerated, dangling jewelry or loud, flashy ties.

4. Practice and arrangements

Using the following practice and arrangement techniques will improve your nonverbal delivery.

Practice techniques Here are some possible practice techniques.

- *Avoid reading or memorizing.* You won't be able to establish eye contact or rapport if you are reading; you won't have time to memorize every presentation. Instead, practice speaking conversationally, referring to your notecards as necessary.
- *Rehearse out loud on your feet.* Knowing your content and saying it aloud are two completely different activities, so do not practice by sitting and reading over your notecards. Instead, practice out loud and on your feet. For an important presentation, rehearse the entire thing out loud and on your feet. For a less important presentation, practice the opening, closing, and main transitions out loud and on your feet.
- *Memorize three key parts.* Another suggestion is to memorize your opening, closing, and major transitions. These are the times when speakers feel the most nervous and are most apt to lose composure.
- *Practice with your visuals.* As we discussed on page 136, become familiar with your equipment; make sure it works and you know how to use it smoothly. Practice to integrate what you are saying with what you are showing and to avoid delivery problems such as talking to the screen.
- *Improve your delivery.* While you're practicing, you can work to improve your delivery by videotaping your rehearsal, by practicing in front of a friend or a colleague, or by speaking into a mirror to improve your facial expression or an audiotape recorder to improve your vocal expression.
- *Simulate the situation.* You might try practicing in the actual place where you will be making the presentation or in front of chairs set up as they will be when you speak.
- *Time yourself.* When you practice, you should also time yourself to avoid the common problem of going overtime. Time yourself honestly: say the words as slowly as you would in conversation, not as quickly as you would read them; actually take the time to change your slides or flip your charts. If your presentation is too long, edit it. If your real presentation runs overtime, you run the risk of getting cut off in the middle or of irritating your audience.

Arrangement reminders In addition to practicing, another way to gain confidence is to make the necessary arrangements for your presentation so that you won't be flustered upon discovering your computer doesn't work or you have too few chairs. All the work you do to create a presentation may be wasted if you haven't made such arrangements. Remember that you are responsible for your own arrangements. Although the janitor, your secretary, or the audiovisual technician can help you out, you are the one who will be suffering in front of the audience if arrangements go awry.

You will deliver your presentation more effectively if you do not arrive at the last moment. Get there about 30 minutes early to check the arrangements, fix anything that may be wrong, get comfortable with the place, and mingle with the audience.

- *Room:* First, double-check your room arrangements. Make sure that you have enough chairs, but not too many. Get rid of extras in advance; people don't like to move once they're seated. Make sure that the chairs are arranged as you want them and that any other items you ordered are there and functioning. Check the lighting, ventilation, sources of noise, and any other potential distractions. (If, despite your best efforts, a distraction occurs during the presentation, don't get flustered or pretend it's not happening. Deal with it as naturally as you can.)
- *Visual aids:* Second, check your visual aid arrangements. Make sure that all the equipment and accessories you ordered have arrived. Test all the equipment far enough in advance so that you can get someone to fix or replace it if necessary. Get the number to call if something should break down during your presentation. Test the readability of your slides or handwriting by viewing them from the farthest chair or asking someone seated in the back row. Make sure that every person in the audience will be able to see your visuals. Finally, check the sequence of your slides and handouts.
- *Yourself:* Finally, arrange yourself (as it were). Set up your notecards and anything else you might need, such as a glass of water. Remember that you are "on stage" from the moment the first person arrives. Prepare yourself physically and mentally by using one of the specific relaxation techniques described on the following six pages.

5. Physical relaxation

When speaking in front of a group, most people feel a surge of adrenaline. In fact, fear of public speaking ranks as Americans' number-one fear—ahead of both death and loneliness. Since most people experience this burst of adrenaline, the trick is to get that energy working for you instead of working against you by finding an effective relaxation technique. Experiment with the various methods explained on the next six pages until you find the one or two techniques that are most useful for you.

The first set of relaxation techniques is based on the assumption, shared by many performers and athletes, that by relaxing yourself physically, you will calm yourself mentally.

Exercise. One way to relax is to exercise before a presentation. Many people calm down following the physical exertion of calisthenics, jogging, tennis, or other athletic activities.

Try progressive relaxation. Developed by psychologist Edmund Jacobson, progressive relaxation involves tensing and relaxing muscle groups. To practice this,

- Set aside about 20 minutes of undisturbed time in a comfortable, darkened place where you can lie down.
- Tense and relax each muscle group in turn. To tense a muscle group, clench vigorously for a full five to seven seconds. To relax a muscle group, release the tension very quickly and enjoy the warmth of relaxation. The muscle groups are hands, arms, forehead, neck and throat, upper back, lower back, chest, stomach, buttocks, thighs, calves, and feet.
- Repeat the procedure at least twice, tensing and relaxing each group of muscles in turn.
- Check your body to find if any areas still feel tense; repeat the tension-and-relax cycle in those areas.

Use the Sarnoff squeeze. Speech coach Dorothy Sarnoff advocates this technique.

- Inhale through your nose; exhale through your mouth, making a "sssss" sound and contracting the abdominus rectus muscles, what Sarnoff calls the "vital triangle" just below the rib cage.

Relax specific body parts. For some people, stage fright manifests itself in certain parts of the body—for example, tensed shoulders, quivering arms, or fidgety hands. Here are some exercises to relax specific body parts.

- *Relax your neck and throat.* Gently roll your neck from side to side, front to back, chin to chest, or all the way around.
- *Relax your shoulders.* Raise one or both shoulders as if you were shrugging. Then roll them back, then down, then forward. After several repetitions, rotate in the opposite direction.
- *Relax your arms.* Shake out your arms, first only at the shoulders, then only at the elbow, finally letting your hands flop at the wrist.
- *Relax your hands.* Repeatedly clench and relax your fists. Start with an open hand and close each finger one by one to make a fist; hold the clench; then release.

Relax your voice Sometimes nervousness shows itself in the voice. Symptoms include cracking, quivering, and dry mouth. Here are warm–up exercises and some general techniques for keeping your voice in shape.

- *Exercises to warm up your voice:* (1) Humming: Hum slowly and quietly—never forcing the voice—for greater volume. Also, hum with a full range of pitches to open up a greater range for you to use when you start speaking. (2) Breathing: Practice controlled inhalations and exhalations. The exhalation may be a series of short, staccato bursts of air, or one long, continuous stream of air released as slowly as possible. Throughout the exercise, you should focus on the basics of correct breathing, expanding and contracting your lower diaphragm, not your upper chest.
- *Techniques to keep your voice in shape*: In addition to vocal warm–up, here are some general suggestions for keeping your voice in shape: (1) Wake up two or three hours before you have to speak to provide a natural warm–up period for your voice. (2) Take a hot shower to wake up your voice or to soothe a tired and irritated set of vocal cords. Steam is very soothing and will help your vocal cords shed any mucus or phlegm that has built up on them. (3) Avoid consuming milk or other dairy products before you speak. Dairy products tend to coat the vocal cords, and this may cause problems during your presentation. (4) Drink any warm liquid to soothe a tired voice. Ideal candidates are tea and coffee. (5) Get enough rest the night before your presentation; sufficient rest is the best guarantee of a good vocal performance.

6. Mental relaxation

Some speakers prefer mental relaxation techniques—to control physical sensation mentally. Here are various mental relaxation techniques to try until you find one that works for you.

Think positively. Base your thinking on the Dale Carnegie argument: To feel brave, act as if you are brave. To feel confident, act as if you are confident.

Repeat positive words or phrases. Fill your mind with positive words or phrases, such as "poised, perfect, prepared, poised, perfect, prepared."

Think nonjudgmentally. Describe your behavior ("I notice a monotone") rather than judging it ("I have a terrible speaking voice!") Then change the behavior by thinking rationally or using a positive self-picture, both of which are described next.

Think rationally. Avoid being trapped in the "ABC's of emotional reactions," as developed by psychologist Albert Ellis.

1. Here are the ABC's of emotional reactions:
   - A: Activating Event (such as a nervous speaking gesture) sparks an irrational
   - B: Belief System (such as "What a disaster!" or "I must be absolutely perfect in every way; if I'm not perfect, then I'm terrible" or "It's a terrible catastrophe if something goes wrong") which causes
   - C: Consequences (such as, anxiety or depression).
2. Transcend these ABC's by
   - D: Disputing irrational belief systems with rational thought (such as "Now that I'm aware of that gesture, I can gradually eliminate it" or "I don't demand perfection from other speakers" or "My equipment just broke, but that's not the end of the world. I'll go on naturally instead of getting flustered.")

Try visualization. Relax by conjuring up in your mind a visual image of a positive and pleasant object or scene.

- *Imagine a scene.* On each of the several days before the presentation, close your eyes and imagine a beautiful, calm scene, such as a beach you have visited. Imagine the details of temperature, color, and fragrance. If your mind wanders, bring it back to your scene. Concentrate on the image and exclude all else. Try repeating positive phrases, such as "I feel warm and relaxed" or "I feel content."

- *Juxtapose the stress.* A few days before the presentation, visualize the room, the people, and the stresses. Then distance yourself and relax by visualizing this pleasant image. This technique decreases stress by defusing the situation in your mind.

Use a positive self-picture. Many speakers find that positive self-pictures work better than positive words.

- *Visualize yourself as a successful speaker.* Pretend you hear positive comments or applause. Act out this visualization in your head. Then act out the role of the person you've been visualizing.
- *Use a positive video picture.* Work with a videotape of yourself giving a real or simulated presentation. Freeze the video at the point where you really like yourself, where you look and sound strong. Then carry that picture around in your head. When it's time for the next presentation, recreate that person.
- *Think of yourself as the guru.* Remind yourself that you know your subject matter.

Connect with the audience. Try to see your audience as real people.

- *Meet them and greet them.* When people are arriving, greet them, get to know some of them. Then, when you're speaking, find those people in the audience and feel as if you're having a one-to-one conversation with them.
- *Remember they are individuals.* Even if you can't greet the people in the audience, think of them as individual people, not as an amorphous audience. As you speak, imagine you are conversing with them.
- *"Befriend" the audience.* Picture yourself in your own home, enthusiastically talking with old friends. Try to maintain a sense of warmth and goodwill. This altered perception can not only diffuse your anxiety, but also increase your positive energy.

Transform negative to positive. Consider the adrenaline that may be causing nervous symptoms as a positive energy. All speakers may feel butterflies in their stomachs; effective speakers get those butterflies to fly in formation, thereby transforming negative into positive energy.

7. Last-minute relaxation

When it's actually time to deliver the presentation, here are a few relaxation techniques that you can use at the last minute—and even as you speak.

Last–minute physical relaxation Obviously, you cannot start doing push-ups or practice humming as you're sitting or standing there, about ready to begin speaking. Fortunately, however, there are some other techniques that you can use to relax your body at the last minute—techniques no one can see you using.

- *Isometric exercises:* Clench and then quickly relax your muscles. For example, you might press or wiggle your feet against the floor, one hand against your other hand, or your hands against the table or chair; you might clench your fists, thighs, or toes. Then quickly relax the muscles you just clenched.
- *Deep breathing exercises:* Inhale slowly and deeply from the diaphragm, then exhale slowly and completely. Pause between breaths. Try breathing in through your nose and out through your mouth. Or, try imagining you are breathing in "the good" and breathing out "the bad." Avoid hyperventilating or shallow breathing from your upper chest.

Last-minute mental relaxation Also at the last minute, you may dispel stage fright mentally by using what behavioral psychologists call "internal dialogue," which means, of course, talking to yourself. Here are some examples:

- *Give yourself a pep talk.* "What I am about to say is important" or "I am ready" or "They are just people."
- *Play up your audience's reception.* "They are interested in my topic" or "They are a friendly group of people."
- *Repeat positive phrases.* "I'm glad I'm here; I'm glad you're here" or "I know I know" or "I care about you."

As you speak Finally, here are four techniques that you can use to relax even as you speak.

- *Speak to the interested listeners.* There are always a few kind souls out there who nod, smile, and generally react favorably. Especially at the beginning of your presentation, look at them, not at the people reading, looking out the window, or yawning Looking at positive listeners will increase your confidence. Soon you will be looking at the people around those good listeners and ultimately at every person in the audience.
- *Talk to someone in the back row.* At the beginning of the presentation, take a deep breath and talk to the person in the back row to force breathing and volume.
- *Remember that you probably look better than you think you do.* Your nervousness is probably not as apparent to your audience as it is to you. Experiments show that even trained speech instructors do not see all the nervous symptoms speakers think they are exhibiting. Managers and students watching videotapes of their performances regularly say, "Hey, I look better than I thought I would!"
- *Concentrate on the here and now.* Focus on your ideas and your audience. Forget about past regrets and future uncertainties. You have already analyzed what to do: now just do it wholeheartedly. Enjoy communicating your information to your audience, and let your enthusiasm show.

II. CONSULT/JOIN NONVERBAL SKILLS

NONVERBAL SKILLS		
Section in this chapter:	**I. Tell/Sell Nonverbal Skills**	**II. Consult/Join Nonverbal Skills**
Who speaks most:	You	Your audience
Purposes:	To inform or To persuade	To understand
Typical situations:	Tell/sell presentations	Questions and answers Consult/join meetings One-to-one conversations

In the first part of this chapter, we looked at nonverbal delivery skills to use when delivering a presentation. In this second section, we will consider a second set of nonverbal skills: the nonverbal listening skills used in consult/join situations.

Various studies show that businesspeople spend 45 to 63 percent of their time listening, yet as much as 75 percent of what gets said is ignored, misunderstood, or forgotten. Why? In part, because most of us have had little or no training in listening; because we can think at least four times faster than someone can talk; and because sometimes it's hard to avoid jumping to conclusions or becoming defensive before we've heard the other person out.

By learning to listen well, you will not only receive and retain better information, but you will also be more persuasive, because you will satisfy your audience's desire to be heard and you will improve your rapport and your audience's morale.

The following framework for improving listening skills is adapted from listening expert Robert Bolton. The three listening skills clusters include (1) attending skills, (2) encouraging skills, and (3) following skills.

1. Attending skills

The term *attending skills* means giving physical attention to the speaker—"listening" with your body—either one-on-one or with a group. These techniques will, of course, vary in different cultures.

Posture of involvement To look involved, your posture should look relaxed, yet alert. Maintain an open position, with your arms uncrossed. Do not stay rigid or unmoving; move in response to what the speaker is saying. When seated, lean forward toward the speaker, facing him or her squarely. One technique to show interest nonverbally is to mirror the same degree of formality in your posture as the other person is using.

Eye contact Eye contact also signals interest and involvement. Maintain steady, comfortable eye contact for a few seconds, then gaze around the speaker's face to "read" his or her expression, then back to the eyes. Do not glance toward distant objects, which signals noninterest. Avoid such obvious signs of rudeness as looking at your watch or gazing out the window.

Distance Sit or stand at the appropriate distance from the speaker—neither too close nor too far apart. Cross-cultural expert Edward Hall has identified zones of space in Anglo-American culture: eighteen inches to four feet is "personal space"; zero to eighteen inches is "intimate space." But perhaps the best way to judge distance is by awareness of the audience comfort level: if the other person is leaning away, you're too close; if leaning toward you, you may be too far away. When seated, remember that the head of the table is associated with dominance, and that sitting beside someone may be perceived as cooperative, while sitting across from someone may be perceived as competitive. In one-to-one situations, avoid standing or sitting at a higher level than the speaker.

Eliminating barriers To give your undivided attention, try to remove any possible distractions. In your office, for example, you might have your calls held, close your door, and come out from behind your desk. In a group situation, you might come out from behind a podium or table. In addition, remove any mental barriers: for example, don't think about other tasks, make plans, or daydream.

2. Encouraging skills

In addition to using nonverbal attending skills, use the following three "encouraging skills" to let the other person speak and to avoid speaking too much yourself.

Door openers *Door openers* are nonjudgmental, reassuring ways of inviting other people to speak if they want to. For example, "All right. Let's hear what the rest of you have to say about this" or "You look upset. Care to talk about it?" In contrast, typical door closers include the following:

- *Criticizing:* "You get all upset no matter what we do!"
- *Advising:* "I was upset when I first heard of this too, but all you have to keep in mind is..."
- *Overusing logic:* "I don't see what you have to look so upset about. These numbers speak for themselves..."
- *Reassuring:* "Don't worry; I'm sure you'll understand after you hear..."
- *Stage-hogging:* Responding to someone's else's story by telling one of your own. Even if you are trying to show understanding, they will often feel one-upped.

Open-ended questions One of the main ways to get people to talk is to ask them good questions. The questions designed to elicit the most information from others are known as "open-ended questions"—that is, questions that cannot be easily answered with a "yes" or "no." For example, you are likely to get more extensive responses if you

Ask	*Instead of*
Tell me about the computer project.	Is the computer project going well?
What concerns you about the deadlines on this schedule?	Can you meet the deadlines on this schedule?
How shall we solve this problem	Do you like my solution?

Attentive silence and attention Perhaps the hardest listening skill of all is simply to stop talking. Effective listeners must learn to be comfortable with appropriate silence. Silence gives the other person time to think and to set the pace. Hear the speaker out, even if the message is unwelcome. Instead of talking or interrupting, show your interest by nodding your head and using "minimal encouragers," such as "I see," "Yes," or "Uh-huh."

3. Following skills

Paraphrasing content Paraphrasing means restating the other person's ideas accurately and concisely. This will enable you to check the accuracy of what you think you have heard, encourage the other person to elaborate on what he or she has said, and show that you are listening. Listen for main ideas, patterns, and themes, and organize those main thoughts as you listen, rather than judging or evaluating first. Then restate a few key words or summarize the key thoughts or idea. For example, "So, it sounds as if you are making three suggestions..." then list them or "Seems as though your major concern here is...."

Paraphrasing feelings In addition to hearing what the person says, be sensitive to how she or he says it. Listen "between the lines." Be aware of the speaker's tone of voice, volume, facial expression, and body movement. Examples of paraphrased feelings include "You sound upset about the new policy" or "You seem discouraged about the way your team is getting along" or "Looks like you're pleased with those results."

Note taking or recording You may wish to take notes as you listen to show you are really interested and planning to follow up. In one-to-one situations, explain why you are taking notes, limit yourself to very few notes, so you don't lose your sense of connection; consider sharing the notes as a summary. In a group situation, take notes on your visual aids as explained on pages 139–141.

Sometimes, however, note taking may be inappropriate. Gauge the situation to determine whether taking notes will make the speaker feel policed or whether you will concentrate too much on writing. Sometimes showing your concern with full eye contact is more important than recording the facts.

See checklists on the following pages for a summary of all the skills covered in the previous three chapters, those used for (1) tell/sell presentations (structure, visuals, and nonverbal delivery) and (2) consult/join meetings (what you say, what you record on visuals, and nonverbal listening skills).

TELL/SELL PRESENTATION CHECKLIST

1. Verbal structure: what you say
See Chapter V

1. *Presentation structure (pages 86–89):* Was your presentation structured effectively: opening, preview, clear main points, closing?
2. *Outline (page 90):* Did you prepare an outline rather than a manuscript?
3. *Questions and answers (pages 91–94):* Did you decide when and how to take questions, and answer difficult questions effectively?

2. Visual aids: what you show
See Chapter VI

1. *Presentation as a whole (pages 110–115):* Were your visuals well designed for the presentation as a whole: agenda chart, support charts, "stand-alone sense," transitions between charts?
2. *Each individual chart (pages 116–131):* Was each individual chart well designed: graphic charts to show quantitative data, diagrams to show nonquantitative concepts, word charts to show main ideas, typography readable, color effective, avoiding overload and chartjunk?
3. *Equipment (pages 132–135):* Did you choose the appropriate equipment from among multimedia projection systems, still projection systems, animated projection systems, boards and charts, handouts?
4. *Usage (pages 136–138):* Did you use and interact with your visuals effectively?

3. Nonverbal delivery skills: how you look and sound
See Chapter VII

1. *Body language (pages 144–145):* Was your body language effective: posture, movement, gestures, facial expression, and eye contact?
2. *Vocal qualities (page 146):* Were your vocal qualities effective: inflection, rate, lack of fillers, and enunciation?
3. *Space and objects (page 147):* Did you use space and objects around you effectively: seating, height and distance, and objects?
4. *Practice technique:* Did you use one or more of the practice techniques listed on page 148 and make the arrangements listed on page 149?
5. *Relaxation technique:* Did you use one or more of the relaxation techniques listed on pages 150–155?

CONSULT/JOIN MEETING CHECKLIST

1. Group facilitation skills: what you say
See Chapter V

1. *In advance (pages 96–97):* Did you prepare in advance by setting the objective, selecting the participants, and setting the agenda?
2. *During the meeting (pages 98–101):* Did you facilitate participation during the meeting by delegating tasks, opening and closing effectively, and encouraging others throughout the meeting?
3. *Decision making and follow-up (pages 102–103):* Did you make a decision effectively? Did you plan to follow up with a permanent record and an action plan?

2. Group facilitation skills: what you record
See Chapter VI

1. *Recording techniques:* Did you use the techniques listed on pages 139–141 to plan, possibly use a scribe, and record comments effectively?
2. *Equipment (pages 132–135):* Did you choose the appropriate equipment?

3. Group facilitation skills: nonverbal listening skills
See Chapter VII

1. *Attending skills (page 157):* Did you use effective attending skills: posture of involvement, eye contact, distance, elimination of barriers?
2. *Encouraging skills (page 158):* Did you use effective encouraging skills: door openers, open-ended questions, attentive silence, and attention?
3. *Following skills (page 159):* Did you use effective following skills: paraphrasing content, paraphrasing feelings, note taking or recording if appropriate?

APPENDIX A

Formats for Memos, Reports, and Letters

Effective strategy and writing skills (Chapters I through IV) will work in any of the three standard business formats, so memorizing format rules is not essential. In addition, most companies provide their own memo forms and rules for formatting letters and reports. Use the general guidelines in the appendix only if your company does not have its own.

MEMOS

Standard elements of a memo

1. Date
2. "To" heading: reader's name or distribution list
3. "From" heading: your name
4. "Subject" heading: neither too general nor too specific
5. Signature: informal, sign your first name next to the "From" heading; semiformal, sign your initials next to the "From" heading; formal, sign with a closing at the end.

Sample memo formats

To:
From:
Date:
Subject:

Date:
Subject:
To:
From:

Subject:	Date:
To:	From:

REPORTS

Standard elements of a report

Introductory material

- *Cover letter or memo.* Usually includes reason for writing, authorization for the report, goal, scope and limits, acknowledgments, and audience appeals.
- *Title page.* Title (summary of focus, not vague generalization), name and position of writer(s) and reader(s), and the date.
- *Table of contents.* Outlines major sections of the report. Can include preliminary information (numbered with small romans, i, ii, iii), main and secondary sections (pages numbered with arabics, 1, 2, 3), appendixes (usually lettered Appendix A, Appendix B), exhibits (usually numbered Exhibit I, Exhibit II), and list of illustrations.
- *Executive summary or abstract.* Summarizes the main ideas. Should make sense on its own, since many readers will only read this part. Should summarize your conclusions, recommendations, or implementation steps, not just say, "Five conclusions are reached."

Body of the report

- *Introduction.* Builds reader interest, explains why you're writing, previews your organization. (See pages 60-61 for more information on how to write an introduction.) The introduction is not the same as an executive summary or an abstract.
- *Conclusions, recommendations, findings, and methodology*, organized clearly with effective headings and subheadings. (See pages 50-51 for more on headings.)

Supplementary information (optional)

- *Appendixes.* supplementary documents such as tables of data, samples of forms, copies of questionnaires, and financial statements. Your reader should not have to read your appendixes to follow your main points in the report.
- *Exhibits.* supplementary charts and graphs.
- *List of illustrations.*

LETTERS

Standard elements of a letter

Heading: tells where letter came from and when it was written

- Where: on letterhead paper, at least two lines below letterhead; on plain paper, about an inch from top
- What: on letterhead, date only; on plain paper, three lines: two-line return address, then date

Inside address: tells name and address of person to whom you're writing

- Where: at least two lines below date
- What: *usually five lines:* name, title, company or organization, two-line address; *sometimes four lines:* name and title, company or organization, two-line address

Salutation: addresses reader

- Where: below the inside address. Skip one line before and after the salutation; the salutation is followed by a colon (formal) or comma (informal)
- What: Dear Mr. or Dear Ms. or Dear First Name or Dear Title

Subject line (optional): introduces subject

- Where: usually two lines below salutation, centered
- What: phrase to describe subject of letter

Body: discusses subject

- Where: beginning two lines below salutation
- What: as many paragraphs as needed

Closing:

- Where: below the final paragraph. Skip one line before and after the closing.
- What: closing such as

Formal:	Yours truly,
Semiformal:	Sincerely,
Informal:	Cordially,

Signature:

- Where: usually, your signature in ink first, followed by your typed name and title, three to five lines below closing
- What: written signature and typed name and title

Typist's reference (optional):

- Where: at least two lines below your typed name and title
- What: can contain your initials in capital letters followed by typist's initials in lowercase; if the letter contains enclosures, enclosure notation goes next; if you are sending copies of the letter to other people, copy notation goes next

  MM:cb

  Enclosure

  cc: Susan Schwarz

Letter formats

Option 1: Full block format

Begin all lines at the left margin.

Company Letterhead

Date

Name
Company
Address
Address

Salutation:

Masthron oltry sirton yotad newbet ekt sretcatahe. Torom hitwed locial koodreoy awit rof resanture of aylow niote criten? Oterbirln omar knille freb doof noidnc. Rewsna 350 gintheoms apn tom forme rekam hos wolloh littlge.

Gnkid tubo ptematt yan norku now lewner oz reay diboter etaryon sellony oiytf nersow. Soger doef retaw ellsw tnemeo stin yo teicor sretem bptse hilpen. Nthron osltry sirton yotad neewbet ehlt sretcat ahc hitwed hip locial koodreoy. Awit rof resanture ao aylow whit nioteco.

Closing,

Signature

Option 2: Modified block format The date, closing, and signature begin to the right of center. Paragraphs start at the left margin.

Company Letterhead

Date

Name
Company
Address
Address

Salutation:

Masthron oltry sirton yotad newbet ekt sretcatahe. Torom hitwed locial koodreoy awit rof resanture of aylow niote criten? Oterbirln omar knille freb doof noidnc. Rewsna 350 gintheoms apn tom forme rekam hos wolloh littlge.

Gnkid tubo ptematt yan norku now lewner oz reay diboter etaryon sellony oiytf nersow. Soger doef retaw ellsw tnemeo stin yo teicor sretem bptse hilpen. Nthron osltry sirton yotad neewbet ehlt sretcat ahc hitwed hip locial koodreoy. Awit rof resanture ao aylow whit nioteco.

Closing,

Signature

Option 3: Semiblock format The date, closing, and signature begin to the right of center. Paragraphs are indented five spaces.

Company Letterhead

Date

Name
Company
Address
Address

Salutation:

Masthron oltry sirton yotad newbet ekt sretcatahe. Torom hitwed locial koodreoy awit rof resanture of aylow niote criten? Oterbirln omar knille freb doof noidnc. Rewsna 350 gintheoms apn tom forme rekam hos wolloh littlge.

Gnkid tubo ptematt yan norku now lewner oz reay diboter etaryon sellony oiytf nersow. Soger doef retaw ellsw tnemeo stin yo teicor sretem bptse hilpen. Nthron osltry sirton yotad neewbet ehlt sretcat ahc hitwed hip locial koodreoy. Awit rof resanture ao aylow whit nioteco.

Closing,

Signature

APPENDIX B

Unbiased Language

One of the biggest changes in the business and professional environment has been the increasingly diverse work force. Here are some suggestions for avoiding biased language in your business and professional communication.

Racism

1. Avoid any word, image, or situation that suggests that all or most members of a racial or ethnic group are the same.

   Anglos: prim, cold, stuffy, rational
   Asians: sinister, inscrutable, serene, industrious
   Black: childlike, shuffling, lazy, athletic

2. Avoid qualifiers that reinforce racial stereotypes.

You wouldn't say	**So don't say**
Anthony, a well-groomed white man . . .	George, a well-groomed black man . . .

3. Avoid racial identification except when it is essential to communication.

You wouldn't say	**So don't say**
Pat Buchanan, noted white politician, . . .	Willie Brown, noted black politician, . . .

Sexism

1. Avoid terms that use the word "man" to mean "people."

Avoid	**Prefer**
man-made	artificial
man-hour	working hours
workmen's compensation	worker's compensation

2. Avoid job titles that end with the suffix *-man.*

Avoid	**Prefer**
businessman	executive, manager
foreman	supervisor
salesman	sales representative

3. Beware of third-person pronouns. Here are four solutions:

   - **Reword.**

Typically, a manager at XYZ Corporation will call monthly meetings with his staff.	Typically, a manager at XYZ Corporation will call monthly staff meetings.

   - **Recast as a plural.**

Each employee must decide for himself...	Employees must decide for themselves...

   - **Replace** with ***one, you, he*** or ***she, his*** or ***her.***
   - **Alternate male and female examples.**

4. Avoid sexist salutations, such as "Dear Sir" or "Gentleman." Here are four alternatives.

   - **Use a descriptive term.**

     Dear Customer:

     Dear Subscriber:

   - **Use a job title.**

     Dear Sales Representative:

     Dear Investment Manager:

   - **Use formal non-gender-specific salutations.**

     Dear Sir or Madam:
     Dear Recipient:

   - **Use informal non-gender-specific salutations.**

     Dear Reader:
     Greetings:

Bias against the disabled

1. Avoid mentioning an impairment when it is not pertinent.

Avoid	Prefer
The deaf accountant completed the audit.	The accountant completed the audit.

2. Separate the person from the impairment.

Avoid	Prefer
Bob, an epileptic, has no trouble with the new job.	Bob, who has epilepsy, has no trouble with the new job.

3. Avoid using words that would offend you if you were impaired.

Avoid	Prefer
deaf and dumb	hearing- and speech-impaired
fits, spells	seizures, epilepsy
crippled	disabled
spastic/retarded (unless of course, these words are needed to describe a condition precisely)	

4. Emphasize the positive rather than the negative.

Avoid	Prefer
wheelchair bound	uses a wheelchair
cancer victim	cancer survivor

APPENDIX C
Grammar and Usage

This appendix contains an alphabetical listing of common errors and problems in grammar and usage.

Agreement between pronoun and antecedent

1. Make sure that your pronoun agrees with its antecedent. Use a singular pronoun to refer to antecedents such as *person, woman, man, kind, each, either, neither, another, anyone, somebody, one, everybody,* and *no one.*

   Each of the committee members agrees to complete **his** assignment before the next meeting.

   (To avoid possible sexist connotations implicit in the masculine singular pronouns, see page 171.)
2. Use the noun nearer the verb to determine the pronoun for subjects joined by *or* or *nor.*

   Neither Cameron nor Seth has completed **his** (not *their*) memo.

   Either the manager or her subordinates have made **their** (not *her*) group's proposal.
3. Use a singular pronoun for collective nouns.

   The group is preparing **its** (not *their*) statement.

Agreement between subject and verb

1. Make sure that your verb agrees with your subject—which may not be the nearest noun.

   The **risks** of a takeover **seem** great.

   The **risk** of a takeover **seems** great.

2. Use the noun nearer the verb to determine the verb for subjects linked by *or* or *nor, either . . . or,* and *neither . . . nor.*

   Either the Art Department or the Editorial Department **has** the copy.

3. Use a singular verb for collective nouns, such as *group, family, committee.*

   The committee **is** meeting after lunch.

4. Use a singular verb for subjects such as *each, either, another, anyone, someone, something, one, everybody, no one,* and *nothing.*

   Each of us **is** . . .
   Another one of the members **has** . . .
   Either of them **decides** . . .

Comma and dash splices

1. Never put two sentences together separated only by a comma or a dash.

   Incorrect comma splice: The company suffers from financial problems, it has great potential in research and development.

   Incorrect dash splice: The company suffers from financial problems—it has great potential in research and development.

2. Watch out for comma and dash splices especially when you use conjunctive adverbs such as *consequently, hence, however, nevertheless, therefore,* and *thus.*

   Incorrect comma splice: The company suffers from financial problems, however, it has great potential in research and development.

   Incorrect dash splice: The company suffers from financial problems—however, it has great potential in research and development.

3. Separate comma and dash splices with a period, a semicolon, or a subordinator.

   Separated with period: The company suffers from financial problems. However, it has great potential in research and development.

   Separated with semicolon, implying that the two clauses are of equal importance: The company suffers from financial problems; however, it has great potential in research and development.

   Subordinated first clause, implying that the first clause is less important: Although it suffers from financial problems, the company has great potential in research and development.

See also "Run-on sentences."

Dangling modifiers

See "Modifiers."

Dash splices

See "Comma and dash splices."

Fragments

1. Do not carelessly write a sentence fragment as if it were a complete sentence.

   Incorrect fragment, missing a verb: Especially during the October buying season.

   Incorrect fragment, subordinated subject and verb only: When the October buying season arrives.

2. Do use fragments carefully for emphasis, parallelism, and conversational tone.

   Fragments used correctly for emphasis: Out loud. On your feet. With your visual aids.

Modifiers

1. To avoid confusing your reader, place your modifiers as close as possible to the words they modify.
2. Avoid unclear modifiers.

   Unclear: The task force seemed sure **on Thursday** the resolution would pass.

   Clear: **On Thursday,** the task force seemed sure...

   Clear: The task force seemed sure the resolution would pass **on Thursday.**

3. Avoid "dangling modifiers"—modifiers misplaced at the beginning of your sentence. The opening phrase (before the comma) must refer to the subject of your independent clause.

   Wrong: Young and inexperienced, **the task** seemed easy to Lauren. ("The task" is not "young and inexperienced.")

   Right: Young and inexperienced, **Lauren** thought the task seemed easy.

   Wrong: When calling on a client, **negotiation techniques** are important. ("Negotiation techniques" are not "calling on a client.")

   Right: **Salespeople** calling on a client will find **negotiation techniques** important.

Parallelism

Express ideas of equal importance in grammatical structures of equal importance.

- Parallel adjectives

  Wrong: She was sensitive and a big help.

  Right: She was sensitive and helpful.

- Parallel nouns

  Wrong: The new manager is a genius, a leader, and works hard.

  Right: The new manager is a genius, a leader, and a hard worker.

- Parallel verbs

  Wrong: The workers should arrive on time, correct their own mistakes, and fewer sick days will be used.

  Right: The workers should arrive on time, correct their own mistakes, and use less sick leave.

- Parallel bullet points

  Wrong: The president announced plans to
  - trim the overseas staff
  - cut the domestic marketing budget
  - better quality control.

  Right: The president announced plans to
  - trim the overseas staff
  - cut the domestic marketing budget
  - improve quality control.

- Parallel comparisons

  Wrong: First identifying yourself is more effective than to start right off with your sales pitch.

  Right: First identifying yourself is more effective than starting right off with your sales pitch.

- Parallel repeated words

  Wrong: He hands in his payroll sheets, data cards, and his time report on the first of the month.

  Right: He hands in his payroll sheets, his data cards, and his time report on the first of the month *or* He hands in his payroll sheets, data cards, and time report on the first of the month.

Pronoun agreement

See "Agreement between pronoun and antecedent."

Pronoun case

1. Use the proper case form to show the function of pronouns in a sentence.

CASE FORMS

Subjective	I	he/she	you	we	they	who
Objective	me	him/her	you	us	them	whom
Possessive	my (mine)	his/hers	yours	our (ours)	their (theirs)	whose
Reflexive/ intensive	myself	himself/ herself	yourself	ourselves	themselves	

2. Use the subjective case when the pronoun is the subject. Watch out for:
   - Compound subjects

     He and **I** finished the jobs. **We** (not *Us*) managers finished the job.
   - Subject complements

     That may be **she** (not *her*). It was **she who** paid the bill.
3. Use the objective case when the pronoun is the sentence object, indirect object, or object of a preposition. Watch out for
   - Sentence objects

     The auditors finally left **him** and **me** (not *he* and *I*).
   - Prepositions

     Just **between you** and **me** (not *you* and *I*) . . .
   - Whom: Use for the object of the sentence, subordinate clause, or preposition.

     Whom did you contact at ABC Company?

     The new chairperson, **whom** we met at the cocktail party, starts work today.

     For **whom** is the message intended?
4. Use the possessive to show ownership. Watch out for
   - Gerunds (*-ing* verbs used as nouns)

     We were surprised at **his** (not *him*) resigning.

5. Use the intensive and reflexive for emphasis. Watch out for
    - Misuse of *myself:* (Don't use *myself* if you can substitute *I* or *me.*)

      Daniel and **I** (not *myself*) designed the market survey.

      He gave the book to Julia and **me** (not *myself*).

Run-on sentences

1. Never stick two sentences together with a comma, dash, or no punctuation at all.

   Run-on sentence with incorrect comma (comma splice): The company suffers from financial problems, however, it has great potential in research and development.

   Run-on sentence with incorrect dash (dash splice): The company suffers from financial problems—however, it has great potential in research and development.

   Run-on sentence with no punctuation: The company suffers from financial problems however it has great potential in research and development.

2. Separate run-on sentences with a period, a semicolon, or a subordinator.

   Separated with period: The company suffers from financial problems. However, it has great potential in research and development.

   Separated with semicolon, implying that the two clauses are of equal importance: The company suffers from financial problems; however, it has great potential in research and development.

   Subordinated first clause, implying that first clause is less important: Although it suffers from financial problems, the company has great potential in research and development.

Subject-verb agreement

See "Agreement between subject and verb."

APPENDIX D
Punctuation

This appendix contains an alphabetical guide to punctuation.

Apostrophe

1. Use an apostrophe to form the possessive of a noun or a pronoun.
   - For nouns (singular or plural) not ending in an *s* or *z* sound, add the apostrophe and *s:*

     Smith's account
     women's rights
     one's own

   - For singular nouns ending in an *s* or *z* sound, add the apostrophe and *s:*

     my boss's office

   - For plural nouns ending in an *s* or *z* sound, add only the apostrophe:

     The Smiths' account
     four dollars' worth

   - For hyphenated compounds, use an apostrophe in the last word only:

     my mother-in-law'*s* idea

   - Differentiate between individual and group possession:

     Smith and Green's account (joint ownership)
     Smith's and Green's accounts (individual ownership)

2. Use an apostrophe to mark the omission of letters in contractions.

they are	they're
fiscal 1999	fiscal '99

3. Use an apostrophe and *s* to form the plural of lowercase letters and of abbreviations followed by periods. When needed to prevent confusion, use the apostrophe and *s* to form the plural of capital letters and abbreviations not followed by periods.

   b's
   M.B.A.'s
   J's or *Js*
   MBA's or *MBAs*

4. Do not use an apostrophe with the pronouns *his, its, ours, yours, theirs,* and *whose* or with nonpossessive plural nouns.

    Their department contributed the financial data; ours (not *our's*) added the artwork.

5. Do not confuse *its* with *it's* or *whose* with *who's.*

    Its filing system is antiquated. (its filing system = the filing system of it)

    It's an antiquated filing system. (it's = it is)

    She is an accountant **whose** results are reliable. (whose results = the results of whom)

    She is an accountant **who's** reliable. (who's = who is)

Colon

1. Use a colon as an introducer: to show that what follows will illustrate, explain, or clarify. What follows the colon may be a list, a quotation, a clause, or a word.

    The CEO's decision is final: we will maintain an open-door policy with the press.

    The CEO decided we will do the following: generate a list of potential questions, hold practice interview sessions, and give each person individual feedback after the sessions.

2. Use a colon as a separator between a salutation and the rest of the letter, a title and a subtitle, a chapter and verse of the Bible, and the hour and the minute.

    Dear Ms. Wyatt:

    Guide to Managerial Communication: Effective Business Writing and Speaking

Comma

1. Use a comma to separate independent clauses joined by *and, but, or, nor, for.*

   A long independent clause like this one is perfectly fine, but you need a comma before the coordinator and this second independent clause.

2. Use a comma to set off most introductory elements.

   If you find that you have a fairly long introductory element at the beginning of your sentence, use a comma before your independent clause.

   In addition, use a comma after an introductory transition (such as *for example, in the second place, however*).

3. Use a comma to separate items in a parallel series of words, phrases, or subordinate clauses.

   He arranged his pens, pencils, calendar, calculator, and papers on the desk.

4. Use a comma to set off incidental information in the middle of the sentence.

   Incidental information in the middle of the sentence, like this, should be set off with commas.

   Midsentence transitions, moreover, are enclosed in commas.

5. In general, insert a comma whenever you would have a light, natural pause, or whenever necessary to prevent misunderstanding.

Dash

1. Use the dash where you would use a comma when you want a stronger summary or a more emphatic break. Use a dash to emphasize interruptions, informal breaks in thought, or parenthetical remarks—especially if they are strong or contain internal commas.

   Use the dash for a stronger—more emphatic—break.

2. Do not use a dash in place of a period or in place of a semicolon between two independent clauses.

   Do not do this—do not join two complete sentences with a dash.

3. Type a dash—with no space before or after the surrounding words—as two hyphens. Most word processing programs have a keystroke option for creating a real dash.

Exclamation point

Use extremely sparingly to express strong emotions.

Hyphen

1. Use a hyphen between compound adjectives to distinguish between the modifier and the noun.

   high-speed computer
   light-emitting diode

   A hyphen is not necessary if the compound adjectives make up an extremely prevalent term.

   venture capital firm
   virtual reality games

2. Use a hyphen for triple compound adjectives.

   cut-and-paste editing
   ultra-high-density chip

Italics (or underlining)

1. Use italics for titles of separate publications (books, magazines, newspapers, long musical works) and titles of plays, films, and long poems.
2. Use italics for unusual foreign words; words, letters, or numbers referred to as such; and extremely sparingly for emphasis.

Parentheses

1. Use parentheses for unemphatic parenthetical remarks.

   Unlike dashes—which emphasize the importance of what they surround—parentheses minimize the importance (of what they surround).

2. Use parentheses for defining a new term or new abbreviation.

   The Chicago Board Options Exchange (CBOE) provides more liquidity than traditional over-the-counter options markets.

3. Use parentheses to enclose enumerators within a sentence, such as (1) letters and (2) numbers.
4. Punctuate correctly around parentheses.
   - (If an entire sentence is within the parentheses, like this sentence, place the period inside too.)
   - If just part of the sentence is within the parentheses, as in this sentence, place the period or comma outside the parentheses (like this).

Period

1. Use a period to mark the end of declarative sentences.
2. Use a period to mark most abbreviations.
3. Use three spaced periods, called an ellipsis mark, to indicate the omissions of words in a quoted passage. If the omitted material falls at the end of the sentence, the ellipsis should be preceded by a period.

Question mark

Use only after direct questions, not after indirect questions.

> Direct question: What are you doing?
> Indirect question: He asked what I was doing.

Quotation marks

1. Use quotation marks to enclose all direct quotations from speech or writing. Long prose quotations—more than ten lines—are usually set off by single spacing and indentation and lack quotation marks unless these appear in the original.
2. Use quotation marks to enclose minor titles (short stories, essays, short poems, songs, television shows, and articles from periodicals) and subdivisions of books.
3. Use quotation marks to enclose words used in a special sense or quoted from another context.
4. Do not use quotation marks for common nicknames, bits of humor, or trite or well-known expressions.
5. Punctuate correctly around quotation marks.
   - Always place the period and comma within the quotation marks.
   - Always place the colon and semicolon outside the quotation marks.
   - Place the dash, the question mark, and the exclamation point within the quotation marks when they apply only to the quoted matter; place them outside when they apply to the whole sentence.

     He called to say, "Your idea stinks!"
     (punctuation refers to quoted matter only)

     I just can't believe that he called back to say, "Actually, I like your idea"!
     (punctuation refers to the whole sentence)
6. Use single quotation marks to enclose a quotation or a minor title within a quotation.

   "Use single quotation marks when you have a minor title within a quotation, such as 'The Star-Spangled Banner,' in this quoted sentence."

Semicolon

1. Use a semicolon to join two closely connected independent clauses of equal importance.

   A semicolon indicates a close connection between two independent clauses of equal importance; these clauses will not be joined in addition by a coordinator *(and, but, or, nor, for).*

2. Use a semicolon to join two independent clauses even if they have a transitional word between them.

   A semicolon indicates a close connection between two independent clauses of equal importance; **however,** don't forget the use of the semicolon to separate independent clauses with a transitional word between them (like *however* in this sentence).

3. Use a semicolon to separate items in a series when your list contains internal commas.

   Use a semicolon to separate items in a series when your list is complex, containing internal commas; when you need stronger punctuation, in order to show where the stronger breaks are; and when you want to avoid confusing your readers, who might get lost with only commas to guide them.

4. Do not use the semicolon to separate items in a list unless the list contains internal commas.

Bibliography

The bibliography contains only very best books and articles culled from among many others. Some of these articles are "classic"—that is, not recently published but nevertheless crucial—on timeless topics. Others are recent, providing cutting-edge research on more current topics.

Chapter 1: Communication Strategy

Communicator Strategy

French, J. and B. Raven, "The Bases of Social Power," in *Studies in Social Power*, D. Cartwright (ed.). Ann Arbor: University of Michigan Press, 1959.

Kotter, J., *Power and Influence*. New York: The Free Press, 1985.

Pfeffer, J., *Managing with Power: Politics and Influence in Organizations*. Boston: Harvard Business School Press, 1994.

Tannenbaum, R. and W. Schmidt, "How to Choose a Leadership Pattern," *Harvard Business Review*, March–April 1958, 95–101.

Thompson, M., "The Skills of Inquiry and Advocacy: Why Managers Need Both," *Management Communication Quarterly*, August 1993, 95–106.

Audience Strategy

Robbins, S., *Organizational Behavior,* 8th ed. Upper Saddle River, NJ: Prentice Hall, 1998.

Ross, R., *Understanding Persuasion*, 4th ed. Englewood Cliffs, NJ: Prentice Hall, 1993.

Yates, J., "Persuasion: What the Research Tells Us," Cambridge, MA: Sloan School, Massachusetts Institute of Technology, 1992.

Message Strategy

Buzan, T., *The Mind Map Book*. New York: Penguin Books, 1996.

Flower, L. and J. Ackerman, *Problem-Solving Strategies for Writing*, 4th ed. Orlando: Harcourt Brace & Company, 1994.

Minto, B., *The Pyramid Principle: Logic in Writing, Thinking, and Problem Solving*. London: Minto International, Inc., 1995.

Whalen, D., *I See What You Mean: Persuasive Business Communication*. London: Sage Publications, 1996.

Channel Choice Strategy

Coleman, D. and K. Raman, *Groupware: Technology and Applications*. Englewood Cliffs, NJ: Prentice Hall, 1995.

Weatherall, A. and J., Nunamaker, *Introduction to Electronic Meetings*. Hampshire, England: Electronic Meeting Services, 1996.

Culture Strategy

Culturgrams. Provo, UT: Kennedy Center Publications, Brigham Young University, published yearly.

Dodd, C., *Dynamics of Intercultural Communication*, 5th ed. New York: McGraw-Hill, 1998.

Ferraro, G., *The Cultural Dimension of International Business*, 4th ed. Upper Saddle River, NJ: Prentice Hall, 1998.

Munter, M., "Cross-Cultural Communication for Managers," *Business Horizons*, May/June 1993.

Tannen, D., *Talking From 9 to 5: Women and Men in the Workplace: Language, Sex, and Power*. New York: Avon Books, 1994.

Chapters II, III, IV: Writing

Brusaw, A., *The Business Writing Handbook*, 6th ed. New York: St. Martin's Press, 1999.

Fielden, J. and R. Dulek, "How to Use Bottom-Line Writing in Corporate Communications," *Business Horizons*, July–August 1984, 24–30.

Flower, L. and J. Ackerman, *Problem-Solving Strategies for Writing*, 4th ed. Orlando: Harcourt Brace & Company, 1994.

Locker, K., *Business and Administrative Communication*, 4th ed. Burr Ridge, IL: Irwin, 1997.

Minto, B., *The-Pyramid Principle: Logic in Writing, Thinking, and Problem Solving*. London: Minto International, Inc., 1995.

Murray, D., *Write to Learn*, 5th ed. Fort Worth: Harcourt Brace College, 1996.

Robbins, L., *The Business of Writing and Speaking*. New York: McGraw-Hill, 1996.

Strunk, W. and E. White, *The Elements of Style*. New York: Macmillan, 1995.

Williams, J., *Style: Ten Lessons in Clarity and Grace*, 5th ed. Chicago: University of Chicago Press, 1997.

Chapter V, VI, and VII: Presentations

Bolton, R., *People Skills: How to Assert Yourself, Listen to Others, and Resolve Conflicts.* New York: Simon & Schuster, 1986.

Cooper, M., *Change Your Voice, Change Your Life*. Manhattan Beach, CA: Wilshire Press, 1996.

Howell, J., *Tools for Facilitating Meetings*. Seattle: Integrity Publishing, 1995.

Jay, A. and R. Jay, *Effective Presentation*. London: Pitman Publishing, 1995.

Knapp, M. and J. Hall, *Nonverbal Communication in Human Interaction*, 4th ed. Orlando: Harcourt Brace, 1996.

Morrisey, G., *Loud and, Clear: How to Prepare and Deliver Effective Business and Technical Presentations*. Reading, MA: Addison-Wesley, 1997.

Munter, M., "How to Conduct a Successful Media Interview," *California Management Review*, Summer 1983, 143–150.

Sutcliffe, J., *The Complete Book of Relaxation Techniques*. Allentown, PA: People's Medical Society, 1994.

Toogood, G., *The Articulate Executive: Learn to Look, Act, and Sound Like a Leader*. New York. McGraw-Hill, 1996.

Tropman, J., *Making Meetings Work*. Thousand Oaks, CA: Sage Publications, 1996.

Tufte, E., *The Visual Display of Quantitative Information*. Cheshire, CT: Graphics Press, 1992.

White, J., *Color for Impact: How Color Can Get Your Message Across—or Get in the Way*. Berkeley, CA: Strathmoor Press, 1996.

Williams, R., *The Non-Designers Design Book: Design & Typographic Principles for the Visual Novice*. Berkeley, CA: Peachpit Press, 1994.

Zelazny, G., *Say It With Charts: The Executive's Guide to Visual Communication*. Homewood, IL: Dow Jones-Irwin, 1996.

Index

T